Vintage
Farm
Tractors

The Ultimate Tribute
to Classic Tractors

Ralph W. Sanders

an imprint of Voyageur Press

Dedication

To my parents, John N. and Zelda Sanders. Their shining example still lights our paths.

Edited by Michael Dregni
Designed by Andrea Rud
Printed in Hong Kong

97   98   99   00   5   4   3   2

Library of Congress Cataloging-in-Publication Data
Sanders, Ralph, 1933–
      Vintage farm tractors / Ralph Sanders.
          p.   cm.
      Includes bibliographical references and index.
    ISBN 0-89658-280-9
       1. Farm tractors—United States—History.   I. Title.
TL233.6.F37S26 1996
629.225—dc20   96-11995
                          CIP

Published by Voyageur Press, Inc.
123 North Second Street, P.O. Box 338, Stillwater, MN 55082 U.S.A.
612-430-2210, fax 612-430-2211

Please write or call, or stop by, for our free catalog of natural history publications. Our toll-free number to place an order or to obtain a free catalog is 800-888-WOLF (800-888-9653).

Educators, fundraisers, premium and gift buyers, publicists, and marketing managers: Looking for creative products and new sales ideas? Voyageur Press books are available at special discounts when purchased in quantities, and special editions can be created to your specifications. For details contact the marketing department.

Frontis: Farm equipment makers featured their trademarks, slogans, and products on lapel pins, which were popular as advertising items in the 1920s.

Title page: The small 1917 Turner Simplicity 12/20 was made by a Port Washington, Wisconsin, firm that became a part of Allis-Chalmers in 1965. Harvey Jongeling and Kenneth Hoogestraat of Chancellor, South Dakota, owned and restored this pretty Turner-Simplicity.

Permissions
Some of the color photographs in this book were first printed in the DuPont *Classic Farm Tractors* calendars of 1990 through 1993, and are used here with the kind permission of E. I. du Pont de Nemours and Company, Wilmington, Delaware.

Many of the historic engravings used in this book are reprinted from Paul C. Johnson's 1978 book *Farm Power in the Making of America* with the kind permission of the Institute for Agricultural Biodiversity (IAB) of Decorah, Iowa.

More information on most of the tractors and the collectors featured in this book are available on VHS videotape. Seven videotapes featuring the tractor and owners from *Classic Farm Tractors* calendars, 1990 through 1996, can be ordered from Venard Films, Ltd., Box 1332, Peoria, Illinois 61654. Telephone: (309)-699-3911.

Classic Farm Tractors calendars are published by Calendar Promotions, Inc., 1010 South Ninth St., Washington, Iowa 52353.

Contents

1920s Case advertisement

Acknowledgments

Vintage farm tractors from more than a hundred collectors are featured in this book, and these are the people who made it all possible. Their investment of time, loving care, years of experience, and money brought these proud farm machines from the past back to life.

The initial idea to collect classic tractors for a series of calendars began more than eight years ago in the offices of DuPont Agricultural Products as a way to popularize a new soybean herbicide trademarked as Classic. Long-time friend and former co-worker John Harvey sprouted and championed the idea. In early 1989, he said, "Go!," and I launched on a seven-year odyssey crisscrossing the continent to capture these gorgeous old machines on large-format 4x5-inch color transparency film. It has been a joy! It's the greatest project I have worked on in my more than thirty-eight years in photography and journalism. Thanks, John, for choosing me.

DuPont Ag Products and *Classic Farm Tractors* calendar publisher, Calendar Promotions, Inc., of Washington, Iowa, have been most helpful in supporting the on-going documentary effort that produces the calendar upon which this book is based. Thanks!

My special thanks to these tractor owners and their willing helpers who patiently moved, started, moved again, hauled, loaded, washed, polished, painted, and waited with me for the rain to go away and the light to get just right for the photos.

The owners include: Vern Anderson, Lincoln, Nebraska; Ralph and Roy Bailey, Milden, Saskatchewan, Canada; Ford Baldwin, Lonoke, Arkansas; R. Wayne Beckom, Kokomo, Indiana; Dick Bockwoldt, Dixon, Iowa; John Bossler, Highland, Illinois; John Bourque, St. Genevieve, Missouri; Louie Blodgett, Escalon, California; Paul Brecheisen, Helena, Michigan; Robert Brennan, Emmett, Michigan; Edwin Brenner, Kensington, Ohio; Stanley Britton, Athens, Alabama; Richard Brown, Harriston, Ontario, Canada; Leonard Bruner, Rising City, Nebraska; Sid Bryan, Stilesville, Indiana; Dick and Shirley Carroll, Alta Vista, Kansas; John Clow, Centreville, Maryland; Eldon Coates, Zwingle, Iowa; Dick Collison, Carroll, Iowa; Ronald Coy, New Richland, Minnesota; John W. Davis, Maplewood, Ohio; Jake and Jay Dudkewitz, Cochranville, Pennsylvania; Lyle Dumont, Sigourney, Iowa; Lorry Dunning, Davis, California; Victor Duraj, Davis, California; Alvin Egbert, New Bremen, Ohio; David Erb, Vinton, Ohio; Bob Feller, Gates Mills, Ohio; Dave Frayser, Stilesville, Indiana; Alton and Thalua Garner, Levelland, Texas; James Garrod, Sheridan, Indiana; Robert Garwood, Stonington, Illinois; Harold Glaus and Mike Flowers, Nashville, Tennessee; Jeff Gravert, Cental City, Nebraska; Jim Hanna, Rochester, New York; Darius Harms, St. Joseph, Illinois; Dwight Hart, Jackson, Tennessee; Verlan Heberer, Belleville, Illinois; Fred Heidrick, Woodland, California; Dick Heitz, Delphos, Ohio; Roland Henik, Mt. Vernon, Iowa; Tom Hill, Piqua, Ohio; Ronald Hoffmeister, Altamont, Illinois; Gerald Holmes, Janesville, Minnesota; Kenneth Hoogestraat and Harvey Jongeling, Chancellor, South Dakota; James Hostetler, W. Liberty, Ohio; Don & Marty Huber, Moline, Illinois; Perry Jennings, Decatur, Tennessee; Jim Jonas, Wahoo, Nebraska; Ronald Jungmeyer, Russellville, Missouri; Kenneth Kamper, Freeburg, Illinois; Gary Kelechenyi, Escalon, California; Kurt Kelsey, Iowa Falls, Iowa; Warren, Shirley, and Mark Kemper, Wapello, Iowa; Richard Kimball, West Liberty, Ohio; Irvin King, Artesian, South Dakota; Donald Kingen, McCordsville, Indiana; Jon E. Kinzenbaw, Williamsburg, Iowa; Randall Knipmeyer, Higginsville, Missouri; Raymond and Kent Krukewitt, Sidney, Illinois; Kenneth L. Lage, Wilton, Iowa; James Layton, Federalsburg, Maryland; Robert Lessen, Hartsburg, Illinois; Wilbur Lutz, Sinking Spring, Pennsylvania; Ron MacGregor and family, Kippen, Ontario; Hal Manders, Dallas Center, Iowa; Robert Mashburn, Bolton, Mississippi; Dewey and Bud McIlrath, Roseville, Indiana; Dick Meacher, Moose Jaw, Saskatchewan, Canada; Bill and Sam Meeker, North Henderson, Illinois; Wm. G. Menke III, Mentor, Ohio; Richard and Carlene Meyer, Dudley, Massachusetts; Freeman Miles, Dothan, Alabama; Rex Miller, Savannah, Missouri; Loren L. Miller, Clifton Hills, Missouri; Leslie Moffatt, Brighton, Tennessee; Roger Mohr, Vail, Iowa; Laurence Myers, Dallas Center, Iowa; Dale Nafe, Peirson, Iowa; D. Dwight Neer, West Liberty, Ohio; Bud Neubert, Birchwood, Tennessee; Jean Olson, Chatfield, Minnesota; Robert Porth, Regina, Saskatchewan, Canada; Dave and Wayne Preuhs, Le Center, Minnesota; Richard Prince, Conover, Ohio; Steven and Rachel Rosenboom, Pomeroy, Iowa; Bill Ruffner, Bellevue, Nebraska; Jim Russell, Oblong, Illinois; Rick Scheibel, Mascoutah, Illinois; E. F. Schmidt, Bluffton, Ohio; Z. Lee Schmidt, California, Missouri; Howard and Roger Schnell, Franklin Grove, Illinois; Clem Seivert, Granger, Iowa; Jeffrey Serpa, Escalon, California; Laurance and Elizabeth Shaw, Gainesville, Florida; Merrill and Marilyn Sheets, Delaware, Ohio; Lloyd Simpson, Monroe, North Carolina; Richard Sleichter, Riverside, Iowa; Virden and Biron Smith, Findlay, Ohio; Alan Smith, McHenry, Illinois; Kenneth Smith, Caledonia, Ohio; Powell Smith, Shelbyville, Tennessee; Lyle and Kyla Spitznogle, Wapello, Iowa; Roland Spenst, Alsen, North Dakota; Norman Steinman, Bourbon, Indiana; Phil, Bill, and Glen Steward, Springton, Michigan; Thomas Stewart, Woodstock, Ontario, Canada; Richard Stout, Washington, Iowa; Robert H. Tallman, Harbeson, Delaware; Harlan Thompson, Harper, Kansas; James and Terry Thompson, Laurelville, Ohio; Scott L. Thompson, Tremont, Illinois; Richard Vogt, Enid, Oklahoma; Robert and Ken Waits, Rushville, Indiana; David N. Walker, Chillcothe, Missouri; Herbert Wessel, Hampstead, Maryland; Bruce Wilhelm, Avondale, Pennsylvania; Mel and Lois Winter, Minneota, Minnesota; and Frank Wurth, Freebug, Illinois.

The tractor owners generously shared with me a wealth of information about their tractors that has furthered my education in the powering-up of the American farm with the classic farm tractor. I am appreciative . . . and impressed.

I want to thank the Institute for Agricultural Biodiversity (IAB), Decorah, Iowa, for permission to use the beautiful line illustrations from Paul C. Johnson's 1978 book *Farm Power in the Making of America*. IAB runs a conservation program for endangered farm animal breeds. Many of the breeds may be viewed at the institute's Farm Park in Decorah. IAB is located at 730 College Drive, Decorah, IA 52101.

My wife, Joanne, travels with me when her schedule permits and is an expert at keeping her eye on the weather, helping reflect light into the shot, lugging heavy camera equipment, and cleaning tires and wheels. I appreciate her companionship and her unflagging assistance.

We are also grateful to our hosts for those welcome morning cups of coffee and cookies, much-appreciated lunches, and cooling ice tea and lemonade on hot afternoons.

Thanks also to our sons, Scott and Richard, who work with us in our business, Sanders Photographics, Inc. They keep the place running when we're on the road and have assumed an extra load of work in the studio and labs to give me time to work on the book.

Michael Dregni, editorial director at Voyageur Press, first suggested this book based on the *Classic Farm Tractors* calendars of 1990–1996. Thank you, Michael. It has helped me return to, and reflect on, my farm roots.

Ralph W. Sanders
Des Moines, Iowa

1910s Auto-Tractor advertisement
Companies across North America hawked conversion kits and implements to miraculously transform automobiles into crude but hard-working farm tractors. In the 1950s, Jeeps and Land-Rovers were offered with farm implements, keeping alive this early—and odd—tradition.

Chapter 1

In the Beginning

You Need a Tractor Now.
—Fairbanks-Morse Oil Tractor ad, 1910s

1921 Samson Iron Horse
Left: *Whoa there! No tractor so symbolically demonstrates the move from horses to tractors on North American farms as the Samson Iron Horse. In early 1919, General Motors announced the Iron Horse, a light four-wheel-drive cultivating tractor that could be driven from the seat or with reins, as shown by owner Eldon Coates of Zwingle, Iowa. GM created the Iron Horse by combining its Chevrolet engine with a cultivating tractor design called the Jim Dandy, that it purchased.*

1860s Westinghouse Steam Engine advertisement

George Westinghouse & Company of Schenectady, New York, built pioneering threshing machines, horse powers, and early steam engines with upright boiler systems—in fact, Westinghouse's steamer was the market sales leader from the 1840s until 1867. George Westinghouse later invented the air brake, and this firm was the forerunner of today's corporation.

The formation of the universe began with a big bang. Humankind's development of machines of motive power began with a small pop.

The invention of gunpowder in China between 960 and 1200 AD during the Sung Dynasty is said to have put the pop in the internal-combustion engine. The Chinese made explosives from simple compounds such as saltpeter, charcoal, and sulfur. Wrapped tightly in rolled paper, these compounds created the firecracker.

From those early beginnings came the spark of the idea for using confined explosions to do useful work. Other inventors developed the cannon, a confined cylinder into which gunpowder and a projectile could be loaded and fired. The concept of the cannon was soon harnessed for work: The thrust of the cannonball, or piston, was pushed up the barrel or cylinder bore, by an internal explosion. These were small steps, perhaps, but steps that took centuries to master before indelibly leaving their lasting imprint on our technology.

In 1680, Dutch physicist Christiaan Huyghens proposed a gunpowder-powered engine, but this concept had some problems. The explosion made lots of smoke and ash. And the explosions were dangerous. Thus, there was never a useful gunpowder engine—although gunpowder later played a role in early internal-combustion engines as a way to set recalcitrant single-cylinder machines into motion.

Building a Head of Steam

Using the principles of the cylinder and piston, Englishman Thomas Newcomen harnessed steam in 1712 to run an atmospheric engine used to pump water. Scot James Watt continued where Newcomen left off, and in 1769 made steam work in rotary motion. Watt continued improving the machine and made steam engines from 1774 until 1800, when his patents expired. By 1784, the principles of the steam locomotive were worked out by Scot William Murdock using Watt's engines. Development of practical steam railroad locomotives continued with some regularity following 1804, when Englishman Richard Trevithick's steam carriage traveled at speeds of up to 10 mph (16 km/h).

The external-combustion steam engine produced power for stationary applications and offered good possibilities for portable applications, if size and weight were not the most important criteria. Steam powered the middle part of the Industrial Revolution, which began around 1700 and continued until about 1950. With steam power as an alternative to water power, manufacturing was no longer tied to locations on the "fall zone" beside flowing rivers and streams.

Steam power played a key role in the development of the early American transportation system starting in 1807 when Robert Fulton's *Clermont* steamboat began traveling on inland waterways at speeds of 5 mph

1921 Samson Iron Horse controls
Above: *Belt drives with idler pulley tighteners caused skid-steer turning on the Samson Iron Horse. Owner Eldon Coates says the Iron Horse tractors were only made for six months with a mere 757 built. He only knows of four survivors.*

1900s Case Steam Tractor advertisement
Right: *Jerome Increase Case grew his company into the world leader in steam engines beginning in 1844 and up to his death in 1891. The first Case steam engine arrived in 1876. Case steam-engine production peaked in 1912 at the same time as gas-engined tractors began rolling out of Case factories. By 1924, the market for steam power had fizzled out.*

**1890s Dingee
Woodbury Horse Power**

This sweep horse power featured six-horse teams hitched to the wheel-drawn circular unit. The power was transmitted to a threshing machine by a tumbling rod. Early horse powers used a treadmill; the sweep design was the final, most advanced version. But as threshing machines grew in size, many large farmers put their horses to pasture and replaced them with a powerful, expensive steam engine. For smaller farmers—or those who distrusted the Steam Revolution—hay-powered horses continued to power their farms.

The Dingee Woodbury Power.

(8 km/h). By 1819, the first steam-powered ocean crossing was made from Savannah, Georgia, to Liverpool, England, in the converted coastal packet *Savannah*. Shallow-draft side-paddle and sternwheeler steamboats were soon plying the waters of most American rivers providing cargo and passenger transportation for the burgeoning nation.

The railroad steam locomotive quickly followed the riverboat and added land transportation to steam's early success on the water. Beginning in 1829, railroads spread rapidly across the United States and soon knit the country together by rail. The driving of the Golden Spike in Promontory, Utah, in 1869, symbolized the tying together of the eastern and western reaches of the country. It was this transportation link that allowed the swift settlement of the West and kicked off an agricultural revolution the likes of which the world had never seen.

Mechanization Pushes Farm Production

Farm power made the mechanization of agricultural production possible just as the new nation was developing. From the time of the California Gold Rush in 1849, steam power's role expanded as a replacement for human and animal muscle on the farm. After 1892, there was no stopping steam.

Even as steam became king, the idea of power from internal combustion stayed alive. Steam power required massive machines with limited portability; engineers and users dreamed of small engines without steam's handi-

caps. So work began anew, using other combustibles such as coal gas.

Coal gas was not a perfect fuel, but it was relatively clean-burning. The fuel could be introduced in a controlled way into a combustion chamber and then ignited at the right instant to shove the piston back and rotate the crank. Adding the inertia of a flywheel on the crankshaft produced a continuous rotary motion. The internal-combustion engine was on its way.

In 1860 in Paris, France, Jean Lenoir made the first commercially produced internal-combustion engine. It burned city gas and worked well enough, but its efficiency was poor since the fuel-air mixture wasn't compressed before ignition. Working with Lenoir's ideas, German Nicolaus August Otto patented in 1876 an engine with a four-stroke, or four-cycle, concept. Otto's engine ran more efficiently, compressing the fuel-air mixture, thus charging each power stroke with more potential energy. The modern gas engine was born.

Concurrent developments in producing and harnessing electricity were keys to the further development of the gas engine. Dependable, accurately timed electrical sparks got the job done, whereas igniter tubes, hot bulbs, and other early ignition systems lacked precision and effectiveness. Otto's four-cycle engine was licensed for use worldwide. When his patents expired about 1890, many others started making gas engines.

Otto's engine was called a gas engine, not a gasoline engine; that came later. Otto's invention came along af-

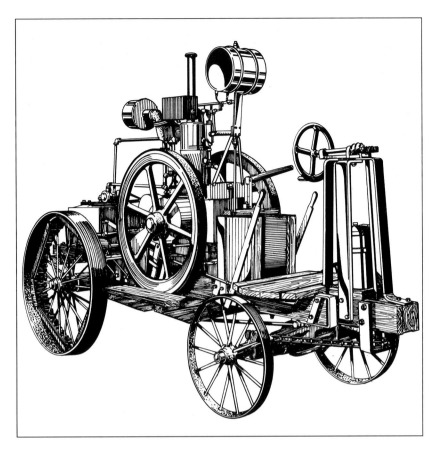

1890s Froelich Gas Tractor

Thresherman and inventor John Froehlich built his own gas-engined tractor in 1892 for threshing work. He mounted a Van Duzen gasoline engine on a Robinson chassis and rigged his own gearing for propulsion. The Froehlich, which became the forerunner of the later Waterloo Boy tractor, is considered the first successful gas tractor.

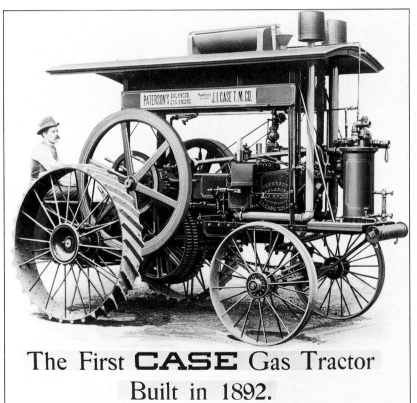

The First **CASE** Gas Tractor Built in 1892.

1890s Paterson Balanced Gas Engine

Engineer William Paterson pioneered gas engines for Case in 1892 or 1894. This early machine apparently did not run well enough to be produced, and Case continued to concentrate on building its monstrous steamers.

ter oil was discovered in Pennsylvania in 1859. Petroleum was first valued for its early use as kerosene, or "coal oil," burned in lamps and stoves. But the early refiners did not know what to do with the smelly gasoline waste product that resulted from refining crude into kerosene and other heavier fuels and oils. Gasoline was often burned as waste or dumped into streams. It was Otto's engine that solved the refiner's dilemma, as gasoline became the preferred fuel for the internal-combustion engine.

Gasoline Comes to the Field

Credit goes to the Charter Gasoline Engine Company of Sterling, Illinois, for first successfully using gasoline as fuel. Charter's creation of a gasoline-fueled engine in 1887 soon led to early gasoline traction engines before the term "tractor" was coined by others. Charter adapted its engine to a Rumely steam-traction-engine chassis, and in 1889 produced six of the machines to become one of the first working gasoline traction engines. Four years earlier in Germany, Karl Benz had already wheeled around in his first three-wheeled automobile; farm tractor technology soon followed the lead of the automotive industry.

Gasoline, although smelly and explosive, was quickly substituted for coal gas in the early engines. Far from uniform in its vaporizing characteristics, early gasoline gave engine developers a hard time. William Paterson, in his early work to give J. I. Case Threshing Machine Company a gasoline tractor in 1892–1894, was only partly successful in mixing gasoline with air for combustion. The first Case gasoline tractor ran, but with carburetion problems and nagging ignition faults it was never developed into a commercially viable machine.

Paterson moved air through a tank partly filled with gasoline and produced an ignitable mixture—sometimes. But since the gasoline lost some of its volatility as it evaporated, poor carburetion resulted. The mixture was too rich, then too lean. In the end, that first Case attempt at a gasoline tractor was put on the back burner for many years until market pressures caused the company to revive the project. By then, others had answered some of the puzzles of carburetion and ignition posed

by the gasoline engine. Venturi carburetors, using physical principals seen at work in perfume atomizers and fly sprayers, coupled with an electrical spark for ignition from magnetos, did the trick.

Froelich Has a Good Harvest

Another branch on the family trees of tractor development started about the same time Paterson was working on the Case machine. John Froelich, a custom thresherman from Iowa, decided to try gasoline power for threshing. He mounted a Van Duzen gasoline engine on a Robinson chassis and rigged his own gearing for propulsion. Froelich used the machine successfully to power a threshing machine by belt during his fifty-two-day harvest season of 1892 in South Dakota.

The Froelich tractor, forerunner of the later Waterloo Boy tractor, is considered by many to be the first successful gasoline tractor known. Froelich's machine fathered a long line of stationary gasoline engines and, eventually, the famous John Deere two-cylinder tractor.

1912 Hart-Parr advertisement
Hart-Parr of Charles City, Iowa, is credited with coining the term "tractor" as well as building the first practical, commercially available gas tractor.

1910s Short Turn tractor
Tractors certainly came in all shapes and sizes in the pioneering years of the 1910s and 1920s. The Short Turn 20/30 was the brainchild of inventor John Dahl and was believed to have been built in both Bemidji and Minneapolis, Minnesota, in 1916–1918.

There were other pioneers as well. Charles W. Hart and Charles H. Parr graduated from the University of Wisconsin in 1896, full of ideas about how the gasoline engine could power agriculture. They experimented with gas engines starting in 1895. By 1902, Hart and Parr built their first tractor, geared for drawbar pulling. Its two-cylinder horizontal engine developed 17 horsepower at the drawbar and 30 hp at the belt pulley at 250 rpm; this subsequently become known in the industry as a 17/30 tractor. Their second model came out in 1903. By 1905, Hart-Parr was operating the first factory in the United States devoted to tractor manufacturing as its sole enterprise.

Tractors in All Shapes and Sizes

During the coming decades, a plethora of people and companies developed tractors. From as few as six known tractor makers in 1904, there were as many as 166 tractor manufacturers by 1920 making a total of more than 200,000 tractors that year.

The result was a great variety of tractor types. At first, they were mostly single-cylinder stationary engines adapted to steam-engine running gears. Next came multiple-cylinder engines, at first mostly twins. Huge flywheels were needed, especially on the single-cylinder engines, to preserve the inertia from the single power stroke every other revolution. Hit-and-miss governors controlled engine rpm by permitting ignition only when the rpm dropped below a preset level.

The early two-cylinder engines came in many styles. Some featured horizontally opposed designs with a cylinder fore and aft of the crankshaft. Others had both cylinders on the horizontal but set parallel to each other. These side-by-side engines differed as well: some had crankshaft throws together so there was a power stroke every revolution, like in the opposed engines; others had the throws offset by 180 degrees for better balance. The offset design gave the Waterloo Boy and later the John Deere two-cylinder tractors their cheery two-pop rhythm, since the two power strokes came one after the other following only 180 degrees of crank rotation.

McCormick-Deering used the double-throw crankshaft with a power stroke each revolution in its popular side-by-side two-cylinder Titan tractor. It sounded smooth, each power stroke coming at 360 degrees of crank rotation—but with both pistons and rods changing directions at the same time, it set up a lively fore-and-aft vibration that could not be balanced at all operating speeds.

Several machines of the early- and mid-1900s used horizontally opposed engines because of their inherently superior balance compared with side-by-side cylinder designs. Avery of Peoria, Illinois; J. I. Case Threshing Machine Company of Racine, Wisconsin; Pioneer of Winona, Minnesota; Universal of Stillwater, Minnesota; and others, used this same design approach. Pioneer's four-cylinder machines were so well balanced that the firm advertised that a nickel placed on edge on a flat

1909 "Minneapolis" Ford

Above: *The 1909 Ford Tractor bears the dubious honor of sparking the Nebraska Tractor Tests. This honor was dubious, at best, because the tractor proved so troublesome to one of its early owners, Nebraska state legislator Wilmot F. Crozier, that he instigated the tests to guard against false and misleading claims made by tractor makers. This Ford Tractor is not to be confused with Henry Ford—although the original company wished it were so. A man named Paul B. Ford beat Henry Ford to the gate with his tractor and incorporated the Ford Tractor Company of Minneapolis before Henry could use the name. Henry Ford subsequently named his tractor the Fordson.*

1915 LaCrosse Happy Farmer advertisement

Right: *The 1910s witnessed an explosion of tractor makes and models with unique, innovative, and even bizarre engineering. The Happy Farmer debuted in 1915, a typical tricycle-style tractor of the era. Unfortunately, not enough farmers were truly happy with the tractor, and the LaCrosse Tractor Company folded in 1922.*

> *This machine will do a hundred other things just like horses do them.*
> *—Bates Steel Mule ad, 1910s*

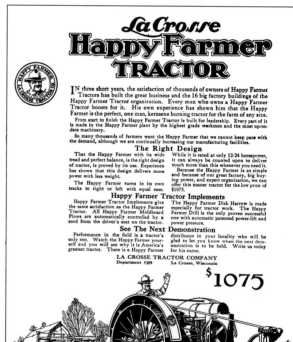

LaCrosse
Happy Farmer
TRACTOR

IN three short years, the satisfaction of thousands of owners of Happy Farmer Tractors has built the great business and the 16 big factory buildings of the Happy Farmer Tractor organization. Every man who owns a Happy Farmer Tractor boosts for it. His own experience has shown him that the Happy Farmer is the perfect, one man, kerosene burning tractor for the farm of any size.

From start to finish the Happy Farmer Tractor is built for leadership. Every part of it is made in the Happy Farmer plant by the highest grade workmen and the most up-to-date machinery.

So many thousands of farmers want the Happy Farmer that we cannot keep pace with the demand, although we are continually increasing our manufacturing facilities.

The Right Design

That the Happy Farmer with its wide tread and perfect balance, is the right design of tractor, is proved by its use. Experience has shown that this design delivers more power with less weight.

The Happy Farmer turns in its own tracks to right or left with equal ease.

While it is rated at only 12-24 horsepower, it can always be counted upon to deliver much more than this whenever you need it.

Because the Happy Farmer is so simple and because of our great factory, big buying power, and expert organization, we can offer this master tractor for the low price of $1075.

Happy Farmer Tractor Implements

Happy Farmer Tractor Implements give the same satisfaction as the Happy Farmer Tractor. All Happy Farmer Moldboard Plows are automatically controlled by a cord from the driver's seat on the tractor.

The Happy Farmer Disk Harrow is made especially for tractor work. The Happy Farmer Drill is the only proven successful one with automatic patented power-lift and power pressure.

See The Next Demonstration

Performance in the field is a tractor's only test. Watch the Happy Farmer yourself and you will see why it is America's greatest tractor. There is a Happy Farmer distributor in your locality who will be glad to let you know when the next demonstration is to be held. Write us today for his name.

LA CROSSE TRACTOR COMPANY
Department #259   La Crosse, Wisconsin

$1075

16

1909 "Minneapolis" Ford
Roland Spenst of Alsen, North Dakota, helped rescue this 1909 Ford from a murky past. He is only the tractor's second owner. This Ford existed as pieces for forty-seven years before Spenst started assembling the old machine. Its crowning moment came when University of Nebraska Agricultural Engineers painted and displayed it at the Tractor Test center in Lincoln, Nebraska, and at the Nebraska State Fair.

part of the frame would remain upright while the engine ran.

Of the hundreds of different engine, transmission, chassis, and wheel designs, relatively few ideas survived the competitive environment; other ideas failed miserably, dragging their inventors down with them. But the larger impact of the keen competition was akin to a nationwide research and development project. Many divergent ideas were tried. Like cream, the good ideas and designs came to the top and were skimmed off as they proved themselves; they were quickly adapted by their originators and adopted by others.

By the early 1920s, many four-cylinder vertical inline engine designs were introduced or already in use. Final drives were fully enclosed in the rear-axle housings. Cooling systems abandoned evaporative cooling for front-mounted radiators with water-pumps circulating the coolant. Air cleaners became common. Crankcases

with pressure circulation of lubricating oil replaced drip lubrication. Ball and roller bearings were used in friction-prone parts. Carburetion problems were worked out and lower-priced kerosene and distillate fuels were burned in most of the machines. The gas tractor was being refined.

Monsters Rumble Along

The first gas tractors were monsters. By 1910, the initial pattern was set: Based primarily on undercarriages designed for steam engines and powered by the huge single-cylinder gas engines of the day, the earliest tractors were large, if not powerful. And, because most tractor makers were expecting their gasoline tractors to replace steam traction engines, the large size was important. The tractors were expected to do heavy tillage work, such as moldboard plowing and other operations needed to prepare soil for planting. The major manu-

1941 Sears Roebuck Economy Tractor

Sears Roebuck and Co. offered this Economy Tractor in its mail-order catalog. The tractor was essentially a converted Ford Model A automobile and was powered by the Ford's engine.

facturers of the day were mostly steam-engine makers hedging their investment in steam with similar-sized gas tractors.

Like the steam engines, the gas tractors had to be suited for belt pulley use to power threshing machines, corn shellers, feed grinders, and other belt-driven equipment. So, for the first ten years of their existence, farm tractors were mostly huge, cumbersome, and expensive behemoths.

This concept began to change after 1910 when smaller and lighter tractors emerged. In 1913, the Bull Tractor Company of Minneapolis introduced its Bull tractor, a lightweight design employing one large drive "bull" wheel on the right, or "furrow" side, and an idler wheel on the left, or "land" side, circumventing the need for a differential. The Bull had a two-cylinder horizontally opposed engine producing 5 drawbar and 12 belt hp. The Bull's three-wheel design aligned the single front wheel with the right driving wheel.

Other similar three-wheelers of the same era included the 1914 Farmer Boy, the 1914 Steel King, the 1914 Allis-Chalmers, the 1915 Happy Farmer, and the 1915 Case 10/20. The Case had an 800-rpm crossmounted four-cylinder engine. The Bull and the other three-wheelers reaped a burst of popularity, but their limitations soon doomed further development and they passed from the scene. Case dropped the three-wheel configuration but kept the crossmounted engine concept alive on its tractors until 1929.

Choosing which tractor to buy from among the hun-

dreds of available brands was another tough row for farmers to hoe. Field demonstrations and trials helped farmers compare the tractors; farm trade magazines sponsored some of the trials, as they still do today. But trials and demonstrations were subject to individual interpretation. Objective help was on its way.

The "Honest" Nebraska Tests

Tractor manufacturers prior to 1920 rated their tractors' drawbar and brake horsepower and advertised and sold tractors based on those ratings. Some early tractors were evidently power-rated by the imagination of advertising copywriters. State legislator Wilmot F. Crozier of Polk County, Nebraska, was so unhappy with his new tractor's performance that he spearheaded a law making tests mandatory. The University of Nebraska developed standardized tests for tractors after the state's Tractor Test Law required tractors sold in that state be tested. Tests began in 1920 and continue today.

The Nebraska testing resulted in many rating changes. Some machines exceeded their claimed horsepower. Others fell short of their power rating and were withdrawn from the test until they could be redesigned or their weaknesses fixed. Sometimes the only "fix" needed was to rerate the horsepower according to the tested output.

The machine that spurred Crozier to create the Nebraska tests was called the Ford tractor. Seeing economic magic in tractors and the name "Ford," promoters in Minneapolis used the name of participant Paul B. Ford to incorporate the Ford Tractor Company. The promoters' goal was not so much to build a better tractor as it was to sell Henry Ford of Model T car fame the rights to his own name for use on his coming tractor. In the end, the "Minneapolis" Ford didn't survive long enough to be tested in Nebraska, and Henry Ford named his machine the Fordson and charged forward.

A Ford in Your Future?

Tractor size and cost all changed suddenly when automobile magnate Henry Ford of Detroit introduced his Fordson tractor in 1917, just as the United States entered World War I. Ford had pioneered assembly-line manufacturing and put America on the road in his Model T Tin Lizzie. His Fordson tractor followed in the footsteps of the Model T.

The Fordson was designed as an inexpensive lightweight machine to replace horses and mules rather than steam engines. It was of standard design with two rear drive wheels and two front wheels aligned with the rear. At 1,000 rpm, its vertical four-cylinder engine fathered 20 hp. Its transmission and rear-axle housing bolted to the engine casting for frameless construction.

The Fordson was right for its time. It sold like hotcakes, and by 1922, Fordson sales amounted to 70 percent of all gas tractor sales in the United States; just a year later, sales peaked at 76 percent of the market. This meant that three out of every four of the 131,908 tractors sold in 1923 were Fordsons.

"Geared to the Ground"

With tractors shedding weight, some makers worried that traction through drive wheels would also decrease. One concept was to put more traction surface on the ground with steel tracks as Holt and Best—later to be amalgamated as Caterpillar—had done in California with their machines. Many small crawler tractors were marketed to address the problem; Cletrac of Cleveland, Ohio, said its crawlers were "Geared to the Ground."

Among the better-known crawlers were the Bates Steel Mule, Bullock Creeping Grip, Yuba, Cletrac, Monarch, Caterpillar, and International Harvester's TracTracTor. Many found their niche in specific applications, such as where soil compaction or soft conditions were a problem. But crawler tractors never sold as well as wheeled tractors for farm use; the additional cost for the track mechanism, as well as extra maintenance of the track and roller mechanisms, deterred cost-conscious buyers.

Lightweight tractors were in by 1915, and tractor makers scrambled to supply the market. The heavy tractors survived in wheat country on the Great Plains where their heavy pulling power was needed to work and seed vast acreages and then run the threshing machines to harvest the crop. But there were still 24,018,000 horses and mules working on U.S. farms in 1923. What a potential market for tractor sales!

The Farmall Weighs In

Ford's market lead started to crumble when another, even better, tractor design caught on. International Harvester Company of Chicago brought out a lightweight tractor in 1924 that even the Fordson could not top. IH's Farmall could literally "farm all." Designed with crop clearance of 30 inches (75 cm), the Farmall's rear wheels were wideset to straddle two 40- to 42-inch (100- to 105-cm) crop rows and its tricycle configuration placed its two front wheels close together so they would fit between the rows. Its two-row cultivator was front-mounted for excellent visibility and precise control from the operator's seat. Cable-actuated wheel brakes let it turn on a dime at row ends to work adjoining rows.

The expansion of corn production had Corn Belt farmers in a quandary. Weed control in row corn called for careful cultivation, usually three times over. The crop was first cultivated down the rows in the direction it was planted. Next it was "cross" cultivated across the rows in the check-row created by hill planting at row width. Then it was "laid by" when it was again cultivated down the planted row when the leaves met between the rows. The custom was to use one- or two-row horse-drawn riding cultivators to get the careful cultivation that good weed control demanded. Operators had to handle the horses with reins in hand, and steer the cultivator blades with their feet.

Horse cultivation was slow, tedious work involving two or three horses pulling a one- or two-row cultivator. By the 1920s, many operators used tractors for most crop operations, but kept horses to cultivate row crops. Some manufacturers offered lightweight cultivating tractors just for cultivating, but many farmers balked at buying another, single-purpose tractor. It was not just sentiment that made many farmers keep their horses and mules.

The Farmall was just what farmers were waiting for. It was lightweight yet powerful enough to pull two plows or other similar-sized equipment for tillage work. It had a belt pulley for powering stationary equipment and a

Rating 12-20

~The most efficient tractor in America~

1920s Bates Steel Mule 12/20 advertisement

Above: *Call them tracklayers, crawlers, or caterpillars, steel-tracked tractors were created to spread the machine's weight over a larger surface, increase traction, and lessen soil compaction. Made by the Joliet Oil Tractor Company of Joliet, Illinois, the Steel Mule may have lived up to its namesake's proverbial stubbornness as it soon disappeared from the market.*

1916 Strait's Tractor advertisement

Right: *The Strait's 30-hp Tractor from Appleton, Wisconsin, boasted a bizzarre blend of a small crawler track to steer the front, a large driven track on the side, and a single support wheel on the other side. As this ad promised, it "never slips— never skids—works in any place every day, rain or shine."*

The new-fangled tractors will be the ruination of the farmer because they don't make no manure.
—Tractor non-believer's proverb, 1920s

30 H. P. Weight 5700 lbs.

STRAIT'S TRACTOR

Will pull two or three 14″ plows. The long chain tread pulls on soft ground or mud where wheel machines fail.

STRAIT'S TRACTOR

never slips—never skids—works in any place every day, rain or shine. Offering a few tractors only on quick orders at $795.00 to advertise; later the price will be $995.00. Write for full information. DO IT NOW.

Killen-Strait Mfg. Co.
Meade St.   Appleton, Wis., U.S.A.

1939 Farmall F-20
The great Farmall arrived in fields in 1924 and almost single-handedly revolutionized agriculture. This dazzling 1939 Farmall F-20 was restored by owner Tom Hill of Piqua, Ohio.

power takeoff (PTO) for running pulled equipment. And with its two-row cultivator, farmers could at last replace their horses and mules with one general-purpose tractor. By 1928, IH had 47 percent of the gas-tractor market; by 1929, its share had risen to 60 percent. It was the Farmall that made the competitive difference and moved IH above Ford in total U.S. tractor sales.

That market dominance impacted all tractor manufacturers, but especially the Fordson. Ford and IH sparked a price war that resulted in Ford selling tractors below production cost. Ford's sales suffered, and, in late 1928, Ford moved tractor production from the United States to the Ford plant at Cork, Ireland; in 1932, the assembly was moved to Dagenham, England. Both models were imported duty free back into the United States.

With ignition systems dating to the Model T, the early Fordsons earned a well-deserved reputation as being temperamental to start. Once they got them started in the morning, many owners let their Fordsons run through noon's mealtime so they wouldn't have the hassle of restarting them. The Irish- and English-made tractors were improved with high-tension magnetos replacing the flywheel dynamo and spark coil on the earlier U.S. tractors. It was 1937 before Ford introduced its row-crop Fordson All-Around, a tricycle tractor with adjustable-tread rear wheels.

Although the Fordson remained in production in England through 1938, it would be more than two decades after the first Fordson was introduced before Henry Ford would make his next major contribution to tractor design.

The Row-Crop Race is On

The success of the row-crop tractor concept, first perfected by IH with its Farmall design, spurred other tractor makers to redesign their smaller machines to achieve similar usefulness and sales popularity. Deere & Company, a relative latecomer to tractor building, chose a three-row design for its first general-purpose machine. Deere's GP was introduced in 1928 as a standard-tread tractor with an upward-bowed front axle built to straddle one crop row and to cultivate three rows. In many respects, the GP was a scaled-down version of Deere's popular Model D, the firm's first all-new tractor design developed after buying the Waterloo Gasoline Engine Company in 1918. The Deere D was introduced in 1923 and soon earned its reputation as a dependable, economical standard tractor.

A mechanical equipment lift on the GP was a John Deere first and was soon emulated by other manufacturers. Although Deere kept the GP three-row in production until 1929, the model did not achieve the market share the company had sought; it was soon replaced with a tricycle-configured wide-tread model, the GPWT. The GPWT had rear wheels spaced far enough apart to straddle two rows and front wheels narrowed to drive down the middle of two rows, much like the Farmall. Deere's GPWT also was designed to front mount a two-row cultivator.

Most of the major tractor makers debuted a row-crop model—either purpose-designed or adapted from an existing design—in the late 1920s and early 1930s. In 1930, Allis-Chalmers adapted its Model U to a tricycle configuration and named it the All-Crop Model UC. Case introduced its tricycle CC general-purpose model. The recently formed Oliver bowed its tricycle row-crop on "tip-toe" steel wheels, based on Hart-Parr and Oliver engineering. Incorporated just one year earlier, Minneapolis-Moline Power Implement Company introduced its Twin City K-T Kombination Tractor. Like the Deere GP, it was a standard tractor with crop clearance built in with an arched front axle and rear geared "drop boxes" to raise crop clearance. It was replaced in 1932 with a tricycle-type row-crop, the M-M Universal.

The Massey-Harris approach was novel for the time. The firm's 1930 General Purpose tractor was a four-wheel drive available in four tread widths for different row spacings. Crop clearance was achieved with drop boxes from both front and rear axles; the front wheels steered through universal joints. It proved to be an idea at least thirty years ahead of its time.

Rubber Hits the Soil

The use of pneumatic, or air-filled, rubber tires on tractors followed the adoption of the general-purpose row-crop tractor by a few years. First seen on tractors around 1932, rubber tires were standard equipment on farm tractors by 1938. During World War II, rubber rationing temporarily returned many of the few tractors produced to steel wheels.

1930s Firestone Ground Grip Tires advertisement

The advantages of rubber-tired tractors were many. As early as 1928, Florida orange growers fastened empty 8x40 truck tire casings to their tractor rims to reduce root damage caused by steel lugs. Tire manufacturers and tractor makers took note; four years later active development of tractor tires was underway.

Firestone Rubber Company worked with Allis-Chalmers to develop rubber tires. The rubber tires were popularized by Allis-Chalmers and Firestone at county and state fairs where famed race-car driver Barney Oldfield burned up the oval horse tracks on a rubber-tired Allis Model U at speeds of more than 60 mph (100 km/h). Goodyear worked with Case on a rubber-tired Model C, and soon Goodrich and U.S. Rubber joined the fray. By 1933, "air tires" were offered on some of the tractors from the nine leading makers.

Scientific field trials of the rubber-tired machines proved better fuel economy at higher operating speeds than that achieved with conventional steel lugs. University of Illinois research showed a 20–25 percent gain in

1930 Massey-Harris GP alongside modern Deere 4WD
Massey-Harris' amazing four-wheel-drive General-Purpose tractor was several decades ahead of its time. Raymond Krukewitt's GP stands alongside one of its engineering ancestors. Raymond's son, Kent, operates the big green machine.

useable drawbar horsepower, with a 25 percent savings in fuel for heavy pulling and an average fuel savings of 14–17 percent for year-round tractor use. University of Nebraska tests compared rubber and steel wheels for cultivating, combining wheat, binding oats, drilling wheat, picking corn, plowing, and moving hay; these tests showed rubber tires resulted in a 13.1 percent savings in time and a 17.9 percent savings in fuel compared to steel wheels.

Although rubber tires added nearly $200 to a new tractor's price, farmers quickly figured the tires would soon pay for themselves in added productivity and fuel efficiency. Iowa State University studies showed that a tractor had to be used just 500 hours per year to recover the cost of rubber tires.

Operators soon learned that additional weight was needed to achieve the best traction from rubber-tired lightweight row-crop tractors. That realization prompted manufacturers to offer optional wheel weights for the rear wheels. Soon, water injected into tires re-placed cast-iron wheel weights. Calcium chloride was mixed with the water to keep it from freezing.

Road travel was greatly enhanced by the rubber tires, and most tractor makers obliged with faster high gears. Tractors were thus made more useful: they could now also pull produce wagons for greater distances in less time.

Gasoline With New Efficiency

By 1935, kerosene and other low-cost distillates had largely become the standard tractor fuel because they cost less per gallon than gas. Up to that year, about 95 percent of tractors were burning kerosene and distillates. Special carburetors were designed to operate at high temperatures to vaporize kerosene and its cousin fuels. But progress in the car world increased engine compression ratios for more efficient power production from gas. Tractor engines were ten years behind car engines in efficiency.

Tetraethyl lead, or ethyl, was being used as an additive to curb gasoline's tendency to pre-ignite and make the engine knock or ping under load. With that problem solved, compressing more fuel and air per cylinder charge increased an engine's power output and fuel efficiency. Another efficiency came when it was no longer necessary to pre-heat air and fuel before combustion, as kerosene carburetors required. Colder air entering the carburetor in gas tractors was more dense and oxygen rich. University of Illinois trials in 1934 of high-compression tractors burning high-octane ethyl-treated gas showed a 32 percent horsepower increase and a 12.4 percent fuel savings compared to kerosene-fueled tractors of the same size.

In 1935, Oliver brought out the first high-compression tractor engine, promising more power and efficiency. The Oliver 70 HC boasted a small-displacement six-cylinder auto-type engine designed to burn 70-octane gasoline. Expecting to sell 2,000 units, Oliver's sales zoomed to 5,000 tractors by mid-February; that success answered the question of whether farmers would buy high-compression gas tractors. Other makers, including Minneapolis-Moline, took note; within five years, fully a third of new tractors sold had high-compression gas engines.

With rubber tires and high-compression engines, tractor makers were able to build tractors that were smaller, lighter, and more powerful and fuel efficient than ever before. A plethora of new designs of both smaller and larger tractors followed in the late 1930s.

Boom and Bust Cycles Impact the Industry

Economic conditions played a large role in the development and acceptance of the gas tractor in its second and third decade of existence. By 1921, there were 186 tractor makers listed with production down to less than 70,000 tractors. Following 1922, the number of manufacturers dropped to thirty-eight in 1930, making about 200,000 tractors a year. The low point came in the depression year of 1932, with only about 20,000 tractors produced. By 1933, only nine principal makers survived: IH, Deere, Case, Massey, Oliver, Minneapolis-Moline, Allis-Chalmers, Cleveland Tractor, and Caterpillar.

Some economic recovery and vastly improved tractors with row-crop design, rubber tires, and high-compression gas engines helped sales increase in the mid-1930s. By 1941, production rose to 342,093 tractors. World War II defense production caused that figure to drop to less than 135,000 tractors in 1943. Postwar figures rose dramatically as U.S. agriculture made up for lost time. In 1948, tractor production reached an all-time peak of nearly 569,000 units, including 39,412 crawlers. By 1949, there were 141 makers turning out more than 400,000 wheel and tracklaying tractors. As the postwar boom slowed and tractor production caught up with demand, tractor makers were thinned dramatically; by 1960, the number of makers had again dropped to nine major players.

Streamlining Comes of Age

Mechanical design and even overall eye appeal continued to develop rapidly into the late 1930s. Many makers took advantage of the talents of industrial designers to add streamlined sheetmetal to their machines. They borrowed some design elements from the car world to produce rounded shapes that gave tractors modern appeal.

In 1938, Minneapolis-Moline's UDLX Comfortractor was the epitome of modern. Beneath its sheetmetal was a rugged tractor, but externally it was a slick, smooth, elegant creation featuring a fully enclosed cab complete with lights, starter, radio, spotlight, windshield wipers, heater, extra seating, and even a horn. Fenders, front to back, covered and smoothed its outline. Its appeal did not, however, change its economics. Priced at nearly twice that of the same tractor without the luxurious amenities, the Comfortractor was not a sales success: only about 150 copies were sold. Less than half that number now exist, making it one of the most coveted of collectible tractors.

In 1937, Deere hired New York City industrial designer Henry Dreyfuss to style its tractor line. By 1938, gracefully rounded louvers enclosed sharp-edged radiators, and other sheetmetal was streamlined, all to add pleasing lines to the Model A and B tractors. The following year, with design help from Raymond Loewy, IH introduced its new line of Farmall tractors including the now-famous M, H, A, B, and MD. They were wonderfully rounded in the front, with sculpted sheetmetal sweeping back to curved fuel tanks before the driver's seat. There were also new designs from Oliver with its 70 Series row-crop machine. And Case debuted its D Series with rounded cast-iron grillwork flowing into the curvaceous hood and top treatment. The modern tractor was emerging.

Ford and Ferguson Change the Mix

Of the changes made by the major makers in the late 1930s none effected tractor design and engineering as much as the innovations introduced in a tractor design announced in 1939. Henry Ford was back in the U.S.

tractor business with the Ford-Ferguson Model 9N.

Built by Ford at Dearborn, Michigan, the 9N incorporated Irish inventor Harry Ferguson's system of integral hydraulics to lift and control implements mounted to a rear three-point hitch. Two lift arms that hinged from near the rear axle mounted implements at the trailing end. A third link, hinged from near the top of the tractor differential, stabilized the three-point mount, and allowed adjustment of the implement angle to the ground.

Although it was still of four-wheel design, and not the tricycle configuration of most row-crop tractors, the new Ford had provisions for adapting to different row-crop widths by reversing its dished rear wheels and sliding out the front wheels on the adjustable front axle. Implements were rear mounted and quickly coupled by pins to the three-point hitch. A steel drawbar element fit into the lift arms for conventional hitching.

The Ford-Ferguson was a light, two-plow tractor aimed at smaller operations, but its design concepts made a heavyweight impact on tractors for many years to follow. In the years after the Ford-Ferguson introduction, almost every tractor maker eventually adopted integral hydraulics and three-point hitches for implement mounting.

The 9N sold well in the early 1940s until war limited production. Introduced in late 1939, the Ford-Ferguson boasted 37,283 tractors sold by the end of 1940. After World War II, the Ford-Ferguson Model 2N found a home on many small, medium, and even large farms. It was considered a handy tractor that the kids or granddad could operate with ease. In the southern United States it eventually replaced many mule teams that had been kept for light work. Many 9Ns and 2Ns are still working on farms and estates despite their age of fifty years or more.

Numerous tractors followed in the Ford-Ferguson's wake. Deere's M arrived in 1947 as a standard row-crop with Quik-Tach implement mounting. IH brought out its one-plow Cub; Massey-Harris had its Pony and Model 20. By 1948, IH's Farmall C with Touch Control hydraulics was available.

The new Oliver 66, 77, and 88 had direct engine-driven PTOs. Allis-Chalmers' low-to-the-ground Model G was designed especially for vegetable production so the operator could carefully guide it over one row of low-growing crop.

Tractors also grew in size and power. Caterpillar introduced a diesel-engined crawler in 1931, its Model 65, the first diesel tractor in the United States. IH was the first in the United States with a diesel wheel tractor, the 1935 WD-40. Deere's first diesel arrived in 1949 as the R; its two-cylinder diesel engine was started with a small gas "pony" engine. Other makers followed with diesel versions of their larger tractors.

The 1950s witnessed the incorporation of integral hydraulic systems and rear-mounted implements onto almost all tractors. Power steering, first offered by outside suppliers, became standard. As farms consolidated into larger units, the horsepower race began as farmers asked for more power to handle larger acreages. Farmer-innovators often led the manufacturers. Tractors were rigged in tandem permitting one man to operate two machines and double work output. Ford V-8 engines were installed in IH F-20 and F-30 tractors, again to boost productivity. Accessory manufacturers offered oversized pistons and sleeves and other power options, including turbochargers, to soup up engines.

Tractor builders soon responded with increased horsepower and productivity in their factory-built machines. Deere's 1959 introduction of the 215-hp, four-wheel-drive, articulated 8010 upped the ante in the horsepower stakes. Considered ahead of its time, the 8010 nonetheless fired the imagination of tractor operators and builders. More horsepower was on the way.

Consolidation of the Tractor Market

By 1950, U.S. farms were populated with nearly four millions tractors. Just a half century earlier there was only a relative handful of tractors at work.

By 1960, the manufacture of tractors in the U.S. was again down to nine major players: Allis-Chalmers, Case, Caterpillar, Ford, IH, Deere, Massey-Ferguson, Minneapolis-Moline, and Oliver. Deere passed IH in farm equipment sales in 1963 to become the industry leader, a position it strongly defends today against a new second-place challenger, the Case Corporation. The decades of the 1970s, 1980s, and 1990s have brought many more changes and consolidations of manufacturers.

The following chapters tell the stories of the major companies, their products, their beginnings, their survival strategies, and the stories of the firms that for some reason did not succeed, did not become adopted, and did not make a major chapter in the history of tractors. Although these orphan companies did not survive time, the firms and their machines nonetheless played an important role in the overall history of farm mechanization and will be best remembered for their triumphs, not their failures.

Vintage Farm Tractor Timeline

960–1200: Gunpowder invented in China about 1,000 years before the present day. The explosive powder is soon used in warfare, although it is only dreamt of as a source of power in helping people work.

1680: Dutch physicist Christiaan Huyghens conceives a gunpowder-powered engine.

1700s: Birth of the Industrial Revolution, beginning in England and soon spreading through Europe and North America. Steam power is developed: First used to pump water from mines, it was modified for rotary power and used in factories to replace water, animal, or human power. Steam power soon freed manufacturers from locating only near water power sources.

1712: Englishman Thomas Newcomen harnesses steam to run an atmospheric engine used to pump water.

1769: Scot James Watt invents the steam engine, making steam work in rotary motion.

1784: Scot William Murdock invents the steam locomotive.

1793: Cotton gin developed by Eli Whitney. The gin soon opened up the eastern United States to textile production. Whitney also pioneered the use of uniform and interchangeable parts in the manufacture of guns, which eased the manufacture and replacement of parts for gun repair.

1800s: Transportation revolution transforms the United States with toll roads, canals, steamships, and railroads. Raw materials could be assembled and finished goods shipped more economically than before. Golden spike linked the west to the east by railroad at Utah's Promontory Point in 1869; prior to completion of the railway wagontrains and ships had to voyage around the Horn from New York to San Francisco.

1831: Cyrus Hall McCormick invents the reaper and transforms grain harvesting. McCormick-Deering and International Harvester spring from his invention.

1837: John Deere (and probably others) develops the scouring steel plow at Grand Detour, Illinois, that plows the heavy prairie soil. Deere's plow was a major improvement to one of the earliest known agricultural machines. The steel moldboard polished, or scoured itself, and let the heavy soils of the prairie slide by rather than stick to the surface. John Deere begins the company that still bears his name.

1841: *Prairie Farmer* magazine starts the spread of practical farming information in Illinois. Other publications in the east had preceded the magazine, but *Prairie Farmer* informed new prairie settlers of developments in their part of the United States.

1842: Jerome Increase Case perfects a combination of thresher and fanning mill in Rochester, Wisconsin, and later begins manufacture in Racine.

1845: Wemple and Westinghouse of Schenectady, New York, receive a patent on their threshing machine and lead in sales until overtaken by Aultman and Taylor Company of Mansfield, Ohio.

1847: Pitts Pattern threshers are built under license in shops from the East to the Midwest.

1849: The California gold rush coincides with the first American use of steam power. Soon after, the Holt brothers move from the east to California to make and sell tools, wheels, and wagons needed by gold miners. Rapid settlement leads to growth in food demand, and California wheat farming creates another market for Holt—the combined harvester or combine, which the Holts modify with a chain drive so it will not scare horse teams. The Holts and the Daniel Best Company later give the world the Caterpillar tractor.

1859: Oil discovered in Pennsylvania. Gasoline becomes a byproduct of kerosene, or coal oil, production. Kerosene, or distillate, is the preferred tractor fuel for years because it costs less than gasoline.

1861–1865: American Civil War strains agricultural production and spurs further mechanization, including the two-wheeled sulky plow. Horses and mules start to replace oxen as the farmer's prime mover.

1876: Nicolaus August Otto, a German shop clerk, receives a patent on his four-stroke gas engine that later becomes the basic design for the internal-combustion engine. Otto's patents expire in 1890, and the race is on.

1877: Thomas Edison invents the phonograph.

1879: Thomas Edison perfects the carbon filament light bulb and in 1892 builds the first large-scale electric generating station in New York City. His direct-current system is soon outmoded by Nikola Tesla and George Westinghouse's alternating-current system.

1885: Germany's Karl Benz drives his three-wheeled automobile. In 1892 in the United States, Albert Duryea goes for a drive in his automobile.

1889: The United States emerges as the world's largest industrial power and demonstrates its strength in the Spanish American War. Holt tractors transport war materiel.

1890s: Steam traction engines begin to be used on large farms not only to power threshing machines but also to plow.

1892: John Froelich of Iowa gives a gas tractor a field test by threshing wheat for a summer-fall season. Froelich's is probably the first practical tractor. Followed quickly by similar tractors from Van Duzen and others, the race is on to develop a better tractor.

1893: Henry Ford of Michigan builds his first auto in his spare time while employed as a mechanical engineer with the Edison Illumination Company. In 1903, Ford founds the Ford Motor Company, and in 1908, the famous Model T is in production. The Model T remains in production until 1927, with a production run of 15 million cars, when the Model A is finally introduced.

1900s: Telephones come to the farm.

1902: Hart Parr makes its first gas-traction engine in Charles City, Iowa. The firm produces a long line of early machines and is credited with coining the word "tractor" in 1906 to describe its gas-traction engines. Oliver Farm Equipment Company is formed in 1929, joining together Hart Parr and other companies.

1903: On December 17, at Kitty Hawk, North Carolina, Wilbur and Orville Wright successfully fly in a powered "heavier-than-air" flying machine. Unable to buy a lightweight gas engine, they make their own.

1914–1918: World War I erupts in Europe, involving Canada early on and the United States in 1917.

1917: Henry Ford's tractor, the Fordson, begins manufacture. It marks a milestone in tractor design, manufacture, and concept. It features frameless construction, is lightweight for its era, is mass-produced using Ford's assembly-line techniques, and is inexpensive compared with most other tractors of the day.

1920: On November 2, radio station KDKA in Pittsburgh announces Warren G. Harding's election as U.S. President. Radio reception is mostly through "tickling a Galena with a Cat's Whisker" on a crystal set and listening through headphones.

1927: On May 20–21, Charles A. Lindbergh flys his monoplane "The Spirit of St. Louis" from New York to Paris, France, in 33 hours, 32 minutes.

1929: Wall Street stock market collapses and the ensuing panic sparks the Great Depression. Agricultural equipment firms are not spared and merge or go out of business. The Minneapolis-Moline Power Equipment company is put together from Moline Implement, the Minneapolis Steel & Machinery, and the Minneapolis Threshing Machine to form Minneapolis-Moline.

1936: Electrical power is available on most U.S. farms as the Rural Electrification Administration (REA) organizes and finances power cooperatives.

1939–1945: World War II is sparked. On December 7, 1941, the United States enters the war after the Japanese bomb Pearl Harbor, Hawaii.

1945: Atomic Bomb is dropped on Hiroshima, Japan, in August, starting the Nuclear Age.

1946: ENIAC, the first truly electronic digital computer, is in operation at the University of Pennsylvania and the Computer Age is born.

1950s: Television comes to the Heartland as TV broadcast stations are built. By 1955, 67 percent of U.S. households have "the box." By 1960, 87 percent have TV "receivers."

1958: Turbine-engined "jet" passenger transports start passenger service in the United States.

1929 Deere GPWT advertisement

Following the Farmall to the fields were tractors from many makers who were hustling to catch up to the revolutionary small row-crop concept. Deere's General-Purpose model was introduced in 1928, soon to be replaced by this GP Wide-Tread model.

27

Chapter 2

Allis-Chalmers

*You & family can find your dream of
happiness in Allis-Chalmers Five-Star
Family Farming.*
—Allis-Chalmers ad, 1941

Above: **1930 Allis-Chalmers U**

1935 Allis-Chalmers WC
Left: *Times were right in the early 1930s for a low-cost row-
crop tractor and Allis-Chalmers' WC filled the bill. The 1934
WC was the first tractor offered on factory rubber, and the
first row-crop tractor so equipped to be tested at Nebraska.
With rubber tires, the WC cost $825 in 1934. This 1935 version
was converted from steel wheels to rubber tires. Brothers
Dewey and Bud McIlrath of Rossville, Indiana, rebuilt this
WC.*

The Allis-Chalmers Company of Milwaukee was not bridled to steam power and thus was right on target with the lightweight 10/18 tricycle tractor it introduced in 1914. Many other tractor makers of the day were still tied to steam-sized monsters meant for the extensive wheat fields of the West and Northwest.

In 1912, former Wisconsin National Guard Brigadier General Otto H. Falk became president of the newly reorganized Allis-Chalmers. Falk was looking for new opportunities for the firm whose history traced back to Milwaukee's Reliance Works flour-milling company, which was founded in 1847. Falk saw the gas farm tractor as an entry into a broadly expanding new market.

The first Allis tractor, the 10/18, had its chance to help replace horse power in mid-America. Its two-cylinder opposed engine turned at 720 rpm, producing 10 drawbar and 18 belt hp. The 10/18 started on gas and burned economical kerosene once the engine warmed up. Its weight of 4,800 lb (2,160 kg) was light by the day's standards. And the 10/18's one-piece heat-treated steel frame was touted in ads as "the only tractor frame with no rivets to work loose—that cannot sag under heaviest strain."

Unfortunately, the 10/18 was A-C's first farm tractor and the firm's marketing efforts were probably not equal to the tractor's potential. A-C was a maker of industrial goods, including flour-milling and sawmill equipment. A-C's 1914 tractor arrived on the market without an established countrywide dealer network for farm sales and service support. A-C made about 2,700 of the 10/18s from 1914 to 1921, not a large run perhaps, but it was a start in a new market.

Some of the early 10/18s were apparently sold direct to farmers. Joseph F. Buchmayer of Johnson County, Iowa, bought his 10/18 through a mail-order catalog in November 1914. It was shipped by rail from the factory in Milwaukee, Wisconsin, to Morse, Iowa. Buchmayer picked up the tractor in April 1915, and drove it 2½ miles

1914 Allis-Chalmers 10/18
Allis-Chalmers' first farm tractor, the 10/18 of 1914, ran on inexpensive kerosene. The small tank on top held gas for starting. The tractor's "armstrong" starter worked off the belt pulley shaft. A light tractor in its day, it weighed but 4,800 lb (2,160 kg). Allis tractors were painted dark green until 1929, when that color gave way to Persian Orange. Collector Richard Sleichter of Riverside, Iowa, owns this connection with Allis' past.

(6.25 km) to his farm. He used it on the farm until 1936, primarily as a power source for feed grinding and light traction work.

Buchmayer's 10/18 was bought forty-five years later by Richard Sleichter of Riverside, Iowa, and restored to operating condition. In 1984, the tractor toured the United States with Sleichter to help A-C celebrate seventy years in the tractor business.

The firm's second-generation tractor was innovative, too. In 1918, A-C introduced a 6/12 tractor that resembled the Moline Plow Company's Universal tractor. The Allis machine had two front drive wheels with an articulated steering arrangement under which implements were attached. Its 800-rpm LeRoi four-cylinder vertical engine was mounted lengthwise. The machine was an attempt at a general-purpose tractor that could be used for cultivation of row crops and other farm work. But the tractor did not last long: A letter from Moline Plow discussing patent infringement may have encouraged A-C to drop the tractor. It was not on the market after August 1923.

In 1919, Allis backed away from the innovative approach and brought out a more conventional tractor, the 15/30, later rerated at 18/30. The tractor was of standard configuration with a four-cylinder vertical inline engine of the firm's own manufacture. Only 1,157 were made from 1919 to 1922, as the post-World War I depression hit and Henry Ford's inexpensive Fordson was taking over the small-tractor market. Production paused in 1922, but by 1929, marking the 18/30s tenth year of production, nearly 16,000 had been manufactured. Production peaked in 1928 with 4,760 units.

Crawlers Climb Aboard

Allis-Chalmers got into the crawler business in 1928 with the purchase of the Monarch Tractor Company of Springfield, Illinois. Monarch originated in Watertown, Wisconsin, in 1914 and started making tractors in 1917. At one time, Monarch tractors were built in plants located in Watertown and Berlin, Wisconsin; Passaic, New Jersey; and Brantford, Ontario. In 1919, the company reorganized as Monarch Tractors, Inc., later becoming Monarch Tractor Corporation in Springfield in 1925.

Monarch made six tractor models of different sizes. Its early models were the Lightfoot 6/10, weighing 3,200 lb (1,440 kg); the Neverslip 12/20 at 6,000 lb (2,700 kg); and the Monarch 18/30 at 7,100 lb (3,195 kg). The Monarch Model D of 1924 was a 60-hp tracklayer weighing 7.5 tons (6,750 kg). It was often equipped with a cab

and a V-shaped snowplow for snow removal from rural roads. At the time of the Allis acquisition, Monarch's largest machine was the 75, which tipped the scales at 11.5 tons (10,350 kg). Crawler tractor production continued at Springfield after the Allis purchase.

In 1929 and 1930, A-C built the 20/35 wheel tractor, which was basically the same as its old 18/30. Some 2,155 of the 20/35s, or Model L, were sold. A smaller standard tractor was introduced in 1921, the 12/20. After testing at Nebraska in 1921, it was rerated as the 15/25. The 15/25 was equipped with a Midwest four-cylinder valve-in-head engine of 4⅛x5¼ inch (103x131 mm) bore and stroke. Built from 1921 through 1927, only 1,705 15/25s were sold.

Persian Orange Brightens the Times

A milestone tractor arrived from Allis just as the Great Depression loomed. It was a tractor as bright and as colorful as the poppies of California—and fast as well.

In 1929, the United Tractor & Equipment Corporation of Chicago was organized from thirty-two independent farm and industrial equipment makers. A-C, a member of the joint manufacturing and marketing group, was contracted to design and manufacture a tractor for the cooperative called the United. The tractor was launched March 1929 at the Southwest Tractor and Road Show in Wichita, Kansas. But United Tractor was short lived, so A-C continued the tractor design as its own Model U.

A 4¼x5-inch (106x125-mm) engine built by Continental of Muskegon, Michigan, powered the original U. The tractor weighed 4,281 lb (1,926 kg) and was rated at 19.28 drawbar and 30.27 belt hp when tested at Nebraska in 1929. The 7,404 Model Us built from 1929 to 1932 had the Continental S-10 flathead engine. Later models were equipped with A-C's UM valve-in-head engine. With a 4½x5-inch (112.5x125-mm) bore and stroke the UM had a displacement of 318 ci (5208 cc) compared with 284 ci (4544 cc) for the Continental. Both engines were designed to run at up to 1,200 rpm.

The U, as well as all A-Cs after 1929, were painted a bright orange called Persian Orange. A-C's tractor department manager Harry C. Merritt wanted to distinguish his firm's tractors from competing makes. The story goes that on a 1929 trip to California Merritt viewed blaze orange wild poppies from miles away. That was the distinction Merritt wanted, and the U was the first model painted the colorful orange. The dark green paint of the past was gone.

1931 Allis-Chalmers Monarch 50

Above: *Steering clutches operated by a steering wheel gave directional control on this 6½-ton (5,850-kg) crawler. The Monarch 50 preceded Allis' redesigned 1934 Model K and KO crawlers. This Monarch was restored by Loren L. Miller of Clifton Hills, Missouri.*

1918 Allis-Chalmers 6/12 advertisement

Right: *A-C introduced its 6/12 tractor in 1918, bearing a close resemblance to Moline Plow's Universal tractor. The Allis machine had two front drive wheels with an articulated steering arrangement under which implements were attached. The 6/12 was a short-lived attempt at a general-purpose tractor that could be used for row-crop cultivation and other farm work.*

Allis-Chalmers
Farm Tractors

The 6-12
GENERAL PURPOSE
for Cultivating,
Plowing, Seed-
ing, Binding,
Mowing, Rak-
ing and all
other farm
work.

$1,500,000 Have Been Spent in the Past Four Years to make Allis-Chalmers Farm Tractors Right for You

The reputation of the Allis-Chalmers tractor as one of undoubted merit, unqualified efficiency and unquestioned value, is the backbone of our policy.
—Allis-Chalmers ad credo, 1920s

1930 Allis-Chalmers U

Above: *Not a speed demon on steel lugs, Allis' Model U did break tractor speed marks when equipped with pneumatic tires. Allis cast its own name in the radiator tank, and named the tractor the U after the firm for which it was initially designed, United Tractor and Equipment Corporation, ceased operations. This 1930 U has an optional dress-up kit with black stripes and extra decals. Lee Schmidt of California, Missouri, resuscitated this proud U.*

1916 Rumely All-Purpose 8/16 advertisement

Right: *Advance-Rumely entered the small-tractor market with its 1916 All-Purpose, available in either 8/16 or 12/24 models. The tractors had one drive wheel, a steering wheel, and a support wheel.*

Count the savings in corn and cash.
—*Allis-Chalmers ad, 1955*

"It's just like handling a horse gang"

N OTICE the way the plows are hung on this Advance-Rumely "8-16"—right under and in front of you where you can see what's going on every minute—just the same as if you were sitting on a horse gang.

The "8-16" is a real one-man outfit—tractor and plows are combined in one machine and full control is from the driver's seat. With the "8-16" you can back up with your plows, make short turns and cut square corners.

Kerosene for Fuel
The Advance-Rumely "8-16" burns kerosene in such a way that it *pays* to burn it—not just under ideal conditions, but continuously and at variable loads.

The powerful, four-cylinder, heavy duty motor is Advance-Rumely built throughout.

For Drawbar or Belt
Besides being an efficient and easily handled outfit for plowing, discing, seeding, hauling and other drawbar jobs, the Advance-Rumely "8-16" is as efficient and economical on the belt—for threshing, baling, silo filling, husking, etc.

Detachable Plows
When used for jobs other than plowing you simply detach the plows and plow frame complete—a minute's work only.

A New Small Thresher
You can now get the famous "save-all-the-grain" Rumely Ideal Separator in a still smaller size—the 20x36 Junior Ideal. It is made to be run with a small tractor and is a *real* thresher—designed and built just like the larger Ideals.

Get These Catalogs
We have special catalogs on the Advance-Rumely "8-16" tractor and the new Ideal Junior separator. Just ask our nearest branch office.

ADVANCE-RUMELY THRESHER CO.
LAPORTE   *(Incorporated)*   INDIANA

Battle Creek, Mich.   Des Moines, Iowa
Indianapolis, Ind.   Madison, Wisc.
Peoria, Ill.

ADVANCE-RUMELY

1923 Rumely OilPull

Above: *This 1923 Advance-Rumely OilPull Model G was certainly rugged and massive, two key sales features in the 1920s. Its two-cylinder engine had pistons larger than gallon paint buckets (8x10 inches or 200x250 mm) and could produce 20/40 hp at 450 rpm. It weighed 7 tons (6,300 kg), and was cooled by 17 gallons (64½ liters) of oil. Advance-Rumely was bought by Allis-Chalmers in 1930, seven years after this OilPull was built in La Porte City, Indiana. This tractor is owned by Scott Thompson of Tremont, Illinois.*

1931 Rumely 6A

Left: *This 1931 6A was as advanced as Advance-Rumely's machines ever became. Its six-cylinder Waukesha engine drove the tractor through a six-speed gearbox. Ads touted it as a "4 plow tractor at the weight of a 3, a six-cylinder at the price of a four." Either way, after acquiring Advance-Rumely, Allis only sold the 6A until Rumely inventory was exhaused. Norm Steinman of Bourbon, Indiana, is this tractor's proud owner.*

We know that the tractor is an economic necessity.
—Allis-Chalmers ad credo, 1920s

1938 Allis-Chalmers B
Torque-tube frame construction aided downward vision for better cultivating of the straddled row on the small Model B. This 1938 B had a wide, cushioned seat so the operator could sit on either the left or right to oversee the operation of the 10-hp machine. Rubber tired, the tractor sold for $495—and cost even less when equipped with steel wheels. Dwight Hart of Jackson, Tennessee, brought this one back to life.

Buying Market Share

In June 1931, Allis-Chalmers took over the Advance-Rumely Thresher Company of La Porte, Indiana. The old full-line farm equipment firm had its beginnings in the mid-1850s as M. & J. Rumely, named for Meinrad and brother John Rumely. M. & J. Rumely and its successor firms had pioneered threshing machines, stationary steam engines, portable steam engines, and steam traction engines, as well as the famous line of Rumely OilPull oil and gas tractors.

Advance-Rumely was organized in 1915 after Meinrad consolidated with three old-line equipment makers: Gaar-Scott & Company of Richmond, Indiana, dating to 1836; Advance Thresher Company of Battle Creek, Michigan, founded in 1881; and Northwest

Thresher Company of Stillwater, Minnesota, dating to 1884. In 1924, Advance-Rumely bought Aultman & Taylor Machinery Company of Mansfield, Ohio, another long-time steam-engine threshing-equipment maker dating to pre-Civil War times. Advance-Rumely apparently sold off the Aultman-Taylor inventory of machines without manufacturing replacements. That was one way to handle competition: buy them and bury them.

Rumely had help in developing its famous OilPull from John Secor, an early experimenter with low-cost fuels for internal-combustion engines, and his nephew William Higgins. The duo crafted carburetors to burn distillate; water injection was devised to keep the two-cylinder engines running smoothly on heavy pulls.

By early 1910, the first Rumely OilPull came off the

1915 Aultman-Taylor 30/60
Steam engines were short lived after huge gas-tractor replacements, like this Aultman-Taylor 30/60, rumbled out of the factories. Four 7x9-inch (175x225-mm) cylinders gave it the heart to plow the prairies. Aultman-Taylor was purchased by Advance-Rumely in 1924. Mel and Lois Winter of Minneota, Minnesota, cherish this heavyweight.

production line; in October 1910, the first 100 were built. By the time A-C bought Advance-Rumely in 1931, Rumely had made 56,647 OilPulls in fourteen different models. It had also made 802 Rumely 6A tractors, a standard tractor with a six-cylinder Waukesha engine first introduced in 1930. A-C sold the remaining inventory of 6As after it took control of Advance-Rumely. A-C got the LaPorte plant, some branch houses, the Advance-Rumley line of equipment, and new dealers with its customer base. The LaPorte facilities were to figure prominently in a later A-C success story, the All-Crop combine.

Advance-Rumely also produced the DoAll tractor, a machine derived from a design it bought in 1927 from Toro Manufacturing Company of Minneapolis. Toro's combination tractor and row-crop cultivating machine was an early attempt at a general-purpose tractor. Two Rumely DoAll models were available. One model converted to a motor cultivator by shifting the rear wheels forward and removing the front axle and wheels. A large caster tail wheel attached to the cultivator, then supported the rear of the tractor. Conversion time was estimated at a half day. The 20-hp lightweight machine was also available without the conversion feature. More than 3,000 DoAlls were built by Rumely, but A-C didn't use the Toro design to pursue the row-crop general-purpose tractor market.

Air Tires and Mile-A-Minute Tractors
The Allis Model U played a big role in the development and use of pneumatic rubber tires on farm tractors. As

a Firestone family friend, tractor department head Harry Merritt furnished a U to Harvey Firestone for use on his Homestead farm in Ohio. Firestone was intrigued with the possibilites of using rubber on the farm and cooperated fully with Merritt and A-C in figuring out how to equip tractors with pneumatic tires. Once the major problems were solved, A-C introduced the innovation and demonstrated it publicly near Dodge City, Kansas, on Labor Day 1932. The rubber-tired U had working speeds of 2½ mph, 3⅓mph, and 5 mph (4 km/h, 5.25 km/h, and 8 km/h), and in fourth gear could motor down the highway at 15 mph (24 km/h).

To popularize the concept of rubber-tired tractors, Allis hired professional race drivers to demonstrate them on county and state fair tracks. On September 17, 1933, retired Indy driver Barney Oldfield drove an air-tired U to 64.28 mph (102.85 km/h) on a measured mile course in Dallas, Texas. The first man to drive an auto at more than a mile a minute had repeated his feat years later—on a tractor.

From 1929 through 1953, Allis produced 23,056 Model Us. On steel, the tractor had a three-speed transmission plus reverse. Those factory equipped with rubber had a four-speed transmission plus reverse and could hit the road at 10.75 mph (17 km/h). As a teenager, I fondly recall the sight of an old rubber-tired U swiftly dispatching wagons of baled alfalfa hay from the field where I was firmly seated on the right side (wire-tying side) of a Case pickup baler. There was no wait for empty wagons with the U quickly bounding to and from the barn.

Responding to the success of general-purpose tractors, A-C modified the U as a tricycle and introduced the All-Crop Model UC row-crop tractor in 1930. A few more than 5,000 UCs were built between 1930 and 1941. But the next generation of A-C row-crop tractor was the big success: it would start out as a row-crop built for rubber.

The Depression Fighter

Built primarily from off-the-shelf components, the new two-plow Model WC row-crop was introduced in 1933 with rubber tires—the first tractor to offer rubber tires as standard equipment; steel wheels were optional. An automotive-style transmission was coupled to a truck-type differential. A steel-channel frame kept it light without the need for the heavy castings used in the U and UC for their frameless construction. A-C's timing was right for a small no-frills machine following the Great

1938 Allis-Chalmers B steel wheels
Cast-steel lugs aided traction on the Allis one-ton (900-kg) tractor. Most were sold on rubber tires. Drawbar pull was slightly better than 10 hp.

1941 Allis-Chalmers B advertisement

Depression, and during the WC's production run from 1934 to 1948, some 178,000 were made. Popularity of the WC traced to its no-nonsense design and its price of $675 on steel or $825 on rubber.

In 1935, the hefty Model A was introduced for wheatland farmers. It was a four-plow machine of standard-tread configuration available with a 4¾x6½-inch (119x162.5-mm) engine or a larger 5¼-inch-bore (131-mm) engine that put out 44 belt hp at 1,000 rpm. In the Model M's production run from 1936 to 1942, only some 1,225 were built.

Allis went the opposite direction in size on its next model. The Model B was a small row-crop machine with a bowed front axle and wide-set front wheels built for use on smaller farms. Its 3¼x3½-inch (81x87.5-mm) engine tested out at 12.97 drawbar and 15.68 belt hp at Nebraska in 1938. The Model B was considered a one-plow tractor and was aimed at replacing the team on the family farm. Tread could be adjusted from 40 inches to 52 inches (100 cm to 130 cm) for different row widths. The B remained in production from 1938 to 1957 with some 127,186 units produced. It was available on rubber tires or steel wheels. With lights, starter, muffler, and radiator shutter, the B sold for $570 in early 1941. It set a trend for tractors to come with its torque-tube chassis.

The next model Allis introduced returned to the tricycle-wheel placement for row-crop use. The Model C debuted in 1940 with a wide operator seat that improved positioning of the driver toward either row for better cultivating visibility. Considered a two-plow tractor, the C came with a 3⅜x3½-inch (84x87.5-mm) engine that gave it 18.43 drawbar and 23.3 belt hp. Equipped with air tires, lights, starter, and muffler, it sold for $595 in early l941. The C was a popular tractor and remained in production from 1940 to 1948 with almost 70,000 built. In 1949, a stronger version was produced, the CA. Power was boosted by speeding rpm from 1,500 to 1,650 rpm. From 1949 to 1957, about 38,618 CAs were built.

Smaller Yet
The odd-looking, but useful Model G was introduced by Allis in 1948. Designed for the G's truck farmer, the one-row design put the operator inches above the row being tended. A rear-mounted 10-hp Continental AN-62 pushed the 1,400-lb (630-kg) "hoe on wheels" through the fields at speeds as slow as ¾ mph (1.2 km/h). Wheel tread was adjustable from 36 inches to 64 inches (90 cm to 160 cm). The G's twin-tubular steel

frame provided plenty of visibility for guiding and clearance for mounting a 12-inch (30-cm) plow, cultivator, or other implements. From 1948 to 1955, a total of 29,036 Model Gs were built at Gadsden, Alabama.

Another postwar Allis effort was the Model WD, a worthy successor to the popular WC, with more horsepower and features. First introduced in 1948, the WD was tweaked and re-introduced in 1950. It featured power-adjusted rear-wheel tread achieved by spiral bars on the wheel rims. Operators could spin out the tires to ten possible tread widths set by adjustable stops on the rims. The WD also featured a dual clutch arrangement so tractor forward travel could be halted without stopping the PTO or hydraulic pump.

By 1953, a total of 131,273 WDs had been made, and the WD-45 was announced. Basically the WD-45 was an improved WD with ½ inch (12.5 mm) extra stroke added to the 4x4-inch (100x100-mm) engine of the older tractor. The WD-45 was available with a Liquified Petroleum Gas (LPG) engine. A diesel version with a six-cylinder 230-ci (3680-cc) engine bowed in 1955. It was A-C's first diesel wheel tractor; A-C began building diesel crawler tractors soon after it acquired Monarch in 1928. The WD-45 was the first Allis tractor to offer factory power steering. More than 83,000 gas and diesel WD-45s were sold from 1953 to 1957.

Bigger Horses
"More horsepower!" was the call from North American farmers in the late 1950s. Allis responded with a complete redesign and introduction of its new D Series tractors. The D14 was the first, introduced in 1957. It placed the operator over the differential and introduced Power-Director to the line, which used a conventional foot clutch and a hand-operated lever to slow forward travel and add pulling power. A Roll-Shift front axle used power-steering muscle to help change front-wheel spacing. Rear wheels were set by spinning out the wheels. The D14 gas version tested 34.08 belt and 30.91 drawbar hp in Nebraska in 1957. It was built from 1957 to 1960, when it was replaced with the D15. Production of all D14 versions totaled 22,280 units, with more than 17,000 D14s equipped with Roll-Shift.

In 1958, the D17 made its debut, followed by the D10 and D12 in 1959. That year, Allis made as many as fifty model configurations of the D10, D12, D14, and D17.

The D17 was available for diesel, gas, and LPG. Its 262-ci (4192-cc) engine turned at 1,650 rpm and tested 51.14 belt and 46.2 drawbar hp at Nebraska. The four-

1937 Allis-Chalmers A
A four-bottom plow was an easy pull for the Model A, as it was designed for wheatland uses on the drawbar and belt. Owner Dick Heitz of Delphos, Ohio, now competes in tractor pulls with this machine.

cylinder gas 226-ci (3616-cc) D17 produced 52.7 hp, and the LPG version, 59.79 hp. Production of the D17 totalled 62,540 tractors during its ten-year run. They were painted Persian Orange with silver decals. In 1959, color changes were made to both D17 models. They got black edging around the radiator grills, with three black horizontal bars. By 1960, the entire line was painted a more brilliant orange, referred to as Persian Orange No. 2, with cream wheels, grill, steering wheel, and nameplates.

A-C's D10 and D12 replaced the Models B and CA. The D10 and D12 were built only with adjustable wide-front axles. The light two-plow machines were alike except in wheel tread: the D12 had longer rear-axle sleeves and a wider front-axle section for wider row widths than the D10. Both models tested 28.5 belt and 25.8 drawbar hp at Nebraska from their 138.7-ci (2272-cc), 1,650-rpm Allis engines. Less than 10,000 of the little machines were made. During production from 1959 to 1968, there were 5,304 D10s and 4,070 D12s built.

The End and Future of Allis

Allis progressed from a beginner in the farm equipment business in 1914 to the third largest tractor producer in sales in 1936, with a full line of tractors and implements. A-C's share of total sales grew from only 2.9 percent in 1929 to 11.3 percent of the market in 1936. The increased share was primarily due to the almost instant success of the WC row-crop tractor on rubber and the All-Crop combine, the small 5½-foot-cut (165-cm) machine designed for family farm use. But the competition was still fierce. IH's share stood at 44.7 percent in 1936 (down from 51.8 percent in 1929) and Deere's share was 23.3 percent (up from 20.6 percent in 1929).

The farm crisis of the 1980s took its toll on farm equipment manufacturers, including Allis. In December 1985, tractor production stopped at West Allis, Wisconsin. Allis-Chalmers became Deutz-Allis under the ownership of Klockner-Humboldt-Deutz (KHD) of Cologne, Germany. In 1990, Allis-Gleaner Company (AGCO) bought out Deutz-Allis, and Persian Orange replaced Deutz Green.

1938 Allis-Chalmers WC Wide-Front

Both photos: *Wide front axles on this 1938 WC added to the model's stability on slopes. Low front crop clearance, however, limited its popularity for row-crop work. Just a hint of streamlining shows in the new grill treatment from 1937, but more styling was to follow. Allis mechanic and collector Steve Rosenboom of Pomeroy, Iowa, rebuilt this tractor from its "remains" found in a farm grove. The WC once belonged to his grandfather.*

1948 Allis-Chalmers G
Both photos: *The 1948 A-C Model G was a truck farmer's dream. Seated inches above the crop row, the driver was in command of the careful planting or cultivating of short vegetable crops. Collector Jim Hanna of Rochester, New York, rebuilt this 1948 G to an as-new condition. His G is equipped with a 12-inch (30-cm) one-bottom plow and hydraulic lift.*

1948 Allis-Chalmers G controls

Left: *An abbreviated steering wheel made more space for the operator to get into the Model G's seat. The starter was activated by pulling the ring handle behind the rear seat; the ring was linked directly to the starter switch.*

1957 Allis-Chalmers D17

Below: *The Power-Director hand clutch that provided two speeds in each gear was a popular feature on the Allis D Series tractors. The D was introduced in the late 1950s, providing more power for large farms. This 1957 D17 shows the model's new styling and design. Operator comfort was enhanced by placing the seat forward of the rear wheels. Kenneth Kamper of Freeburg, Illinois, owns this D17.*

Chapter 3

J. I. Case

A Million Farmer-Engineers as
Our Advisors.
—Case ad, 1918

Above: **1939 Case DC**

1936 Case RC
Left: *A new light gray color and over-the-top steering were featured on the 1935 Case Model RC. The RC was designed to compete with the IH Farmall F-12, another light row-crop machine. This 1936 RC replaced mules used on the Mississippi River bottomland acreage farmed by collector John Bourque's father and uncle, who had an operation south of St. Genevieve, Missouri.*

Jerome Increase Case founded his company, the J. I. Case Threshing Machine Company in 1844 and grew it into the world leader in threshing machines and steam engines before his death in 1891. The company he founded brought the threshing machine to the Midwest and built about a third of North American steam traction engines made between 1876 and 1925, which marked the end of steam production. His firm's successor, the Case Corporation, continues today as the second-largest supplier of farm power and agricultural implements in the United States.

Moving from his home in New York state in 1842, Case came to the heart of the new Midwest grain-growing country as a young man of twenty-two. He brought with him six "ground hog" threshers, crude machines with revolving pegged wooden cylinders that threshed grain from wheat as it was hand-fed into the thresher. The wooden contraptions were a vast improvement over hand-flailing grain on a threshing floor. Case's father, Caleb, sold the devices in New York state. Jerome, Caleb's youngest son, apparently bought the machines on credit, possibly from his father.

On his way to Rochester, Wisconsin, from his home at Williamstown, near Rochester, New York, in fall 1842, young Case sold five of his "ground hogs." The sixth machine he kept for himself, first to use for custom threshing, then to rebuild into a machine with more capabilities. The revised machine became the foundation of his business as Case coupled it with a fanning mill and created his first crude threshing machine.

Machines From Racine

In spring 1844, Case successfully demonstrated his unit, and by the end of the year he moved to Racine, Wisconsin, opened shop, and had six machines completed. Employing patent rights bought from other threshing machine makers of the day in combination with his own ideas, Case soon led the field, and his machines won coveted prizes at agricultural expositions.

Power for one of Case's threshing machines was initially supplied by a single horse on a treadmill. Later came "horse-powers," harnessing horse teams behind "sweeps" of revolving levers geared to a turning "tumbling" shaft that powered the ever-improving threshing machine.

The first Case steam engine, now enshrined at The Smithsonian Institution in Washington, D. C., was produced by the company in 1876. The machine was a horse-drawn engine of 10 hp designed to give the horses a break in powering the threshing machines of the day.

Case's portable steam engines became self-propelled shortly thereafter, but they still required a horse team to steer them until they were revised in 1884.

Case steam-engine production peaked in 1912. At the same time, gas-engined tractors began rolling out of Case factories. By 1924, the market for steam power had fizzled, and Case steam-engine production stopped after a total production run of more than 35,000 farm engines.

Case Tries Gas Engines

Case's first pioneering efforts at producing a gas traction engine date to 1894, or maybe earlier, when William Paterson of Stockton, California, came to Racine to make an experimental engine for Case. Case ads in the 1940s, harking back to the firm's history in the gas tractor field, claimed 1892 as the date for Paterson's gas traction engine; patent dates suggest 1894. The early machine ran, but apparently not well enough for it to be produced. Carburetion and ignition devices lagged behind the other mechanisms used and, thus, limited dependability.

Paterson's "balanced" engine design was novel, if not successful. It was a horizontal two-cylinder inline engine with adjoining (but not connected) water-jacketed combustion chambers in the engine center. The engine's crankshaft was connected directly to one piston by connecting rod and indirectly connected to the opposite piston by a walking beam and two parallel-acting connecting rods. William Paterson and his brother, James, shared the original engine patent, dated October 30, 1894.

Case stayed out of the gas-tractor business until 1911 when it returned with its 30/60, which won a first place at the Winnipeg tractor trials of 1911. The 30/60 was a monster of nearly 13 tons (11,700 kg), and was produced from 1912 through 1916. A smaller version, the 12/25, debuted in 1913. A mid-sized 20/40 won Case more gold medals at the 1913 Winnipeg trials. Like many tractors of the era, these three models were powered by two-cylinder opposed horizontal engines. Crankshafts were of 360-degree offset for a power stroke every revolution. Many components of the heavy machines were from Case's steam line, including rear drive wheels, gearing, and hot-riveted frames and chassis.

In less than a decade, Case moved from making massive Steam Era two-cylinder engines to lighter Automotive Era tractors with four-cylinder vertical inline (but crossmounted) engines. Case tenaciously held to its view of the superiority of spur gears over bevel gears

J. I. Case & Co's Almanac for 1878.

SOME OF THE REASONS WHY WE HAVE A SUPERIOR ENGINE.

1878 Case Steam Engine

Left: *J. I. Case boasted a long history of farm power. Case built its first steam engine in 1876. Although the first steamer was portable, this 1878 model was both portable and self-propelled.*

1918 Case 9/18

Below: *Weighing "little more than a team of horses," the Case 9/18 was a great departure from the company's heavier machines. The four-cylinder motor was mounted transversely across the frame, a design Case retained until 1929. Case collector Herb Wessel of Hampstead, Maryland, completely restored this 9/18.*

1925 Case car and 1918 Case 9/18

Right: *Herb Wessel's 1925 Case Model X Suburban Coupe is one of only two known to exist. This car is part of Wessel's extensive Case collection.*

1919 Case 10/18

Below: *The cast-steel frame and cast radiator tank were improvements made to the 1919 Case 10/18. Introduced in 1917, the 10/18 refined the famous Case Crossmount design before its manufacture ended in 1920. This 10/18 is owned by John Davis of Maplewood, Ohio.*

for power transmission until 1929, when the Model L was introduced. Crossmounted engines made bevel gears unnecessary since the engine, drivetrain, and wheels all rotated in one plane.

The first of the Crossmotor design followed two trends of its time: it was three-wheeled, and it was lightweight. The 10/20 Crossmotor was produced starting in 1915. Like other popular makes of the day, it had one large driving "bull" wheel on the right, or furrow side, with its front "steering" wheel aligned with it on the right. The "idler" wheel on the left had no differential, but could be temporarily "clutched" into the live axle for extra pull in tough going.

The 10/20 was a two-plow tractor weighing just over 5,000 lb (2,250 kg), a true lightweight in 1915. Its second-generation overhead-valve four-cylinder engine was the basis for later Crossmotor designs. Production of the 10/20 continued until 1918, and the model continued to be sold from previous production as late as 1924. Some 4,992 three-wheel 10/20s were sold in the United States before the 12/20 Crossmotor replaced it.

The Smaller the Better

With Henry Ford's Fordson gobbling up much of the lightweight tractor market, Case quickly brought out another lightweight, the 9/18 Crossmotor, introduced in early 1916. The 9/18 weighed in at 3,650 lb (1,642 kg)—a little more than a team of horses. It was rated as a two-plow machine and was advertised as being able to handle a small thresher. A few more than 6,000 of the 9/18As and 9/18Bs were made before production ended in 1919. Case's 9/18 was not a big seller compared with the Fordson, but it presaged a complete line of Case Crossmotor tractors; this line eventually grew in size to match the horsepower ratings of the firm's early gas-oil machines.

By 1917, the 10/18 was on the market. Similar to the 9/18B, but with a cast radiator tank and higher engine rpm, the 10/18 surpassed 9,000 units before manufacture ended in 1920.

The Case 15/27 bowed in 1919 and soon became Case's best seller. Rated for three plows, the 15/27 hit a responsive chord with buyers. The 15/27 was the first Case tractor equipped with a PTO. It sold more than 17,600 units before it was replaced with the upgraded 18/32 in 1924.

Also new to the market in 1919 was the 22/40. Of four-to-five-plow power, the 22/40 weighed more than 9,000 lb (4,050 kg). By its production end in 1924, some 1,850 were made. The 22/40 was upgraded to 25/45 in

1925 with few changes.

In 1922, Case replaced its first lightweight three-wheel 10/20 with the 12/20. The 12/20's pressed-steel wheels served as a ready identifier for the 4,230-lb (1,900-kg) cast-frame tractor with valve-in-head engine. The model stayed in production until 1928 when it was redesignated the Model A. Records show 9,237 12/20s were made, making it the second most popular Case Crossmotor model. Unlike the earlier Crossmotors that were green with red wheels, the 12/20 was all gray.

The largest Case gas tractor of the times was the 40/72. During production from 1920 through 1923, only forty-two 40/72s were made. Tested at Nebraska in 1923, the 11-ton (9,900-kg) behemoth produced more than 91 belt hp, a record for the time. But it set another record, too. Its thirsty, kerosene-burning engine gulped down more than 7½ gallons (28½ liters) per hour for a record low 5.61 hp hours per gallon. The giant 40/72 was too much too late. Smaller, more efficient designs were on the way.

The Crossmotor Era Ends

When Leon R. Clausen joined Case as president in 1924, the company was still firmly in its Crossmotor stage. Clausen was previously manufacturing vice president at Deere, were he had pushed successfully for development and manufacture of the popular Model D and had pursued the row-crop GP. IH's Farmall row-crop tractor had just been introduced as well, and Clausen wanted to move Case forward toward modern, row-crop tractors.

By the early 1920s, most tractor firms had already changed to car-type four-cylinder engines aligned lengthwise along the frame. Case's transverse engine mounting with its wide stance clearly wasn't adaptable to row-crop design since the engine had to fit between crop rows. Clausen stopped Crossmotor development soon after he arrived and directed the firm toward newer designs. Those efforts ultimately resulted in the Models L and C and Case's final entry into row-crop machines.

The introduction of the L came in 1929, after nearly five years of development and testing. The L was of standard configuration with a new long-stroke valve-in-head engine. Its four-cylinder 4⅝x6-inch (116x150-mm) motor produced 47.04 hp in a 1938 Nebraska test. Pressure lubrication, as well as enclosed and oil-bathed drive components, kept the machine on the job for many years. The L tractor was a 26/40 to replace its two nearest-sized Crossmotor machines. The new model came out in a new color—gray—instead of the Crossmotors's

dark green. The L was almost an instant success. During its first two years of manufacture, more than 6,000 were made; in the L's ten-year production run, more than 34,000 came down the assembly line.

Row-Crops and Chicken Roosts

Later in 1929, the Model C debuted. Similar in most respects to the L, the C was rated at 17/27 and designed to pull two to three plow bottoms. Modification of the C into the CC (the second C stood for "cultivator") in 1930 finally gave Case a row-crop tractor to compete with the Farmall and other row-crop designs being introduced by competitors. With the popularity of row-crop tractors in the mid-1930s, Case made nearly 49,500 Model Cs; more than 60 percent of them were the row-crop CCs.

The CC introduced the famous "chicken perch," or "fence cutter," steering arm on the tricycle row-crop tractor, a controversial but familiar feature long associated with Case machines. The distinctive row-crop steering roost stayed with the line until 1955.

Long-time Case vice president and chief engineer David P. Davies left his indelible imprint on the new models. His patented enclosed-roller-chain final drive transmitted power from the differential to the sprockets mounted on both rear driving axles. Case tractors used the same roller-chain-drive design in models made well into the 1960s. Davies played a major role in many of the Case tractor projects going back to the Steam Era. He began as a draftsman at Case, and helped prepare drawings for many machines built there, including the short-lived 1894 Paterson gas tractor.

New Shades of Gray

About the time Case zeroed-in on row-crop tractors with its CC, International Harvester threw a curve ball. IH

1929 Case L

Kerosene and distillates were the favorite tractor fuels when the L debuted in 1929. Enclosed final drive with big roller chains were a Case design feature that stayed with the line well into the 1940s. Rated at 26/40 hp, the L was a long-lasting favorite of Case users.

1929 Case L

The Case Crossmount era ended with the introduction of the 1929 Model L. An overhead-valve four-cylinder engine was mounted lengthwise on the frame, setting the trend for future Case tractors. In addition, green was gone and gray became the Case color starting with the Model L. Case collector and historian David Erb of Vinton, Ohio, owns this L.

introduced second-generation row-crop tractors with its simple F-12 Farmall. The F-12 expressed economy from its small four-cylinder Waukesha engine to its large-diameter wheels mounted simply on large-diameter keyed axles. Infinite row-width wheel settings were as easy as loosening a few bolts and sliding the wheels out to a measured setting. And it was inexpensive as well.

Case dealers and salespeople began to complain that they could only sell the CC because IH dealers were sold out of F-12s. Case's need for a smaller, less-expensive row-crop tractor was finally felt in Racine, and a machine was assembled to compete with the little Farmall F-12. In late 1935, the Model RC began production as a Waukesha-powered tricycle row-crop with an over-the-top steering-gear arrangement. The RC's rear end was borrowed from the Case CC drive unit. Case's familiar side-arm steering was added to the RC beginning in 1937.

To distinguish the new machine from the more pow-

erful—and more profitable—CC, the new RC was painted light gray. Case hoped it would not compete with itself for buyers, and instructed salespeople to sell an RC against other manufacturers' tractors, not against the CC.

RC production began in Racine in late 1935, but it was moved in 1937 to Rock Island, Illinois, factory facilities that came with the February 1937 purchase of the Rock Island Plow Company. Nearly 16,000 Models R and RC were built from 1935 through 1940, which marked the end of the R Series production.

The Flambeau Red Series

A standard four-wheel R, RI (industrial), and RO (orchard) were added to Case's line in 1939. By mid-1939, the Rs were streamlined with a rounded sun burst, or wheat sheaf, cast grill as well as a new hood and a new Flambeau Red paint job. Other refinements included rubber tires, lights, and a starter. Many of the R stan-

1935 Case CC

Above: *Row-crop capabilities were added to the Case tractor line in 1930 with the addition of the Model CC, a row-crop version of the standard Model C. Case's side-arm steering was more sensitive in the central part of the steering arc. This 1935 CC is owned by Stanley Britton of Athens, Alabama.*

1936 Case RC

Left: *The Case RC weighed 2,600 lb (1,170 kg) and sold new for about $950. It featured a hand clutch and three forward gears, and tested at Nebraska as an 18/20 hp tractor.*

dards were exported to Canada.

The new DC was introduced in 1939; it was basically a CC with a streamlined cast grill and hood. Its Case engine was a 3⅞x5½-inch (97x137.5-mm) design. A four-speed transmission gave it working speeds from 2½ mph to 10 mph (4 km/h to 16 km/h). The D Series was a popular tractor and was available on rubber tires or steel wheels. Case made more than 100,000 D Series machines between 1939 and 1955; more than half were the row-crop DC.

Joining the DC in 1940 in the row-crop lineup was the two-plow SC. Designed to compete with the new Farmall H, the S Series was a re-engineered and scaled-down DC. Power came from a shorter-stroke, higher-rpm engine than the D. The battery box was moved under the rear of the fuel tank, rather than on top like the D. The S was also well received, and 74,000 of the S and its model variations were made between 1940 and 1955; three-fourths were the row-crop SC.

The rugged L standard remained in the line following its 1929 introduction, and in 1940, with new stream-lined styling including rounded fenders, grill, and hood, it was introduced in Flambeau Red as the LA. The new five-plow tractor was little changed under the skin. The LA still boasted basically the same 4⅝x6-inch (116x150-mm) engine with a slight boost in compression. Magnetos remained standard equipment long after the LA was offered with lights and starter. Records show some 42,000 of the LA and its variants were made from 1940 to 1953.

So Long to the Team—Finally

Still doing well with its larger models, but experiencing some problems with sales of its smallest R Series tractor, Case reluctantly moved toward smaller units. The demand for one-to-two-plow tractors was increasing rapidly as the ultimate replacement for horses and mules. Since its threshing-machine and steam-engine successes, Case had a long history of sales strength in the Great Plains and other extensive farming areas where small grains were grown on large operations. Just the idea of small tractors went against the Case grain, but the firm's own studies showed the need for team-sized tractors, and the competition was already entering the market.

Allis, IH, and Ford brought out one- and two-plow machines in 1938 and 1939. A-C's Models B and C used mostly vendor components to keep down costs, but they were right on target for the emerging market. The Farmall A had an offset design for better operator visibility. The Ford-Ferguson 9N was aimed at the same market. Case got with the program.

Early 1940 saw the introduction of the Case VC. It was a tricyle-type row-crop powered with a Continental engine. The differential and transmission housings and torque tube were built by Case. The Clark Company of Michigan supplied the transmission and differential gears. Metal work was farmed out to local vendors. The VC was joined by V (standard), VI (industrial), and VO (orchard) versions. Priced at $625, the VC—Case's smallest tractor—was finally competitive with other tractors of its size. The V Series was produced from 1940 through 1942, and enjoyed a production run of more than 16,000 units.

In 1942, Case replaced the V Series with the VA Series. One aim of the new model was to build more of the unit in-house to improve profitability. The VAs had a Case-designed engine built by Continental that contained both Case and Continental parts. Once the Rock Island engine plant began operation in 1947, VA engines were built there.

Transmission and differential gearing were of Case design and manufacture. VAC units started rolling off the line in Rock Island about a month before the bombing of Pearl Harbor, December 7, 1941. By mid-July 1942, when war production closed the VA line, more than 8,500 of the little tractors had been built. During the war, only warehouse versions of the VA were produced. Once manufacturing resumed after the end of the war, Case cranked out VAs at a rapid rate. By the end of VA production in 1955, a total of more than 148,000 had been made; more than 60 percent were the VAC row-crop.

1939 Case R Standard
Facing page, top: *By 1939, the Case R had been styled with a curvaceous cast sunburst grill and new sheetmetal, all painted in the new Case color, Flambeau Red. Robert Porth of Regina, Saskatchewan, Canada, restored this steel-wheeled standard version.*

1939 Case DC
Facing page, bottom: *A streamlined cast radiator grill and molded sheetmetal updated the Case row-crop tractor in 1939 to the two-to-three-plow DC. Rubber tires were the DC's usual equipment, but this DC has heavy-duty steel "sand" lugs. The two-row cultivator mounted in the square opening behind the tricycle front on the DC. Case Quick-Dodge steering with its side arm linkage had a variable ratio for quick turning in the center part of the steering arc. A starter and lights were available, as shown on this DC owned by Warren Kemper of Wapello, Iowa.*

Diesels in the Mix

In 1953, Case introduced the diesel-engined Model 500. Its six-cylinder engine put out 56.32 drawbar hp at its Nebraska test. The Case-designed and -built engine used the Lanova power cell concept. Bore and stroke was 4x5 inches (100x125 mm) on a heavily built crank and crankcase designed to handle the stress from the big diesel unit turning over at up to 1,350 rpm. Double disc brakes, electric lights, and electric starting were all standard. The Model 500, with factory power steering was tested at Nebraska. The 500 was the last of the all-Flambeau Red tractors. New paint was on its way.

The 500 was but the first of the new 1950s model introductions. In early 1955, a two-tone Model 400 bowed as the successor to the Model D. It was available in gas, diesel, LPG, or distillate versions in row-crop, regular, orchard, high-clearance, or industrial configuration. Powering the 400 was a four-cylinder version of the 500's engine with power up to 1,450 rpm, 100 rpm more than the 500. Engine and castings on the new model series were painted in Flambeau Red with sheet metal in contrasting Desert Sunset.

Soon joining the two-tone fleet were the Model 300, replacing the S Series in 1956, and the Rock Island–built 200, replacing the VA Series. In 1956, the 500 was upgraded to become the 600, with the new styled grills and two-tone paint of the smaller models.

The Case for Crawlers

Case got into the tracklaying market in 1957 when it bought the American Tractor Corporation of Churubusco, Indiana. The firm's Terratrac models included the gas GT-25 and GT-30 and a DT-34 diesel. Hydraulic lifts, PTO, and six track gauges from 36 inches to 72 inches (90 cm to 180 cm) for different row spacings were available. Case continued production of the crawlers at Churubusco through the 1950s, but in 1961, manufacture was shifted to the Case facilities in Burlington, Iowa.

Emerson-Brantingham Purchase

Acquisitions were not a novelty for Case. One of its largest purchases came in June 1928, when it bought the huge, but financially troubled, Emerson-Brantingham Company of Rockford, Illinois. The addition gave Case a long line of well-known implements, a valuable dealer network, and new sales territory in the heart of the Corn Belt. Like Case, E-B was a pioneer in the field, tracing its roots back to 1852 and John H. Manny's reaper. By the 1910s, E-B was one of the largest ag equipment firms in the United States.

In 1912, E-B purchased the Gas Traction Company of Minneapolis and entered the gas tractor business in a big way with Gas Traction's Big 4 Model 30, a huge 10½-ton (9,450-kg) machine rated at 30 drawbar and 60 belt hp. In 1913, E-B enlarged the Model 30 into the giant Big 4 Model 45. Six cylinders gave the Big 4 Model 45 an expected 45 drawbar and 90 belt hp—and another ton (900 kg) of weight. A smaller Model 20 in 1913, gave E-B a 9,800-lb (4,410-kg) tractor with 20 drawbar and 35 belt hp.

By 1916, E-B had several tractors of its own design, including the firm's popular lightweight Model AA 12/20 of 1918, weighing only 4,750 lb (2,138 kg) and powered by a four-cylinder engine. The AA was further refined in 1925 to become the Model K. In 1923, E-B brought out its No. 101 tricycle two-row Motor Cultivator based on a LeRoi four-cylinder engine. Friction drive gave the No. 101 variable speeds, and a single front wheel steered it down the rows. But motor cultivators were doomed in 1924 when IH debuted the Farmall, so it was not E-B's tractor designs that Case wanted. Case dropped all of E-B's designs in favor of its own machines; rather, E-B's line filled out Case's offering with hay tools, grain binders, and more tillage tools.

Case Buys More History

In 1937, Case purchased the floundering Rock Island Plow Company of Rock Island, Illinois. It, too, was an historic company with roots that reached back to Grand Detour, Illinois, and the steel plow made there by John Deere and others. By 1912, Rock Island Plow had grown into a full-line company offering about anything a farmer might need—except tractors.

Heider Manufacturing Company of Carroll, Iowa, came to the rescue. Henry J. Heider designed a light tractor that used a friction drive in about 1908. Heider's Model A was announced in 1911, soon to be replaced by the Model B of 1912. By 1914, Rock Island Plow was selling Model Bs, and Heider was at work on the Model C. Still of friction-drive design, the C was more conventional in other respects. It was powered by a Waukesha 4½x6¾-inch (112.5x162.5-mm) engine, giving the tractor a four-plow rating. Ground speed was varied by moving the engine forward or backward to change the effective radius of the friction plate where it contacted the engine flywheel.

In January 1916, Heider sold his tractor business to Rock Island, and Henry Heider worked with the plow company to create the Model D in 1917. The Model D

1944 Case LA Standard
Pulling four to five plows was a breeze for the LA, which debuted in 1940. Under its new streamlining and Flambeau Red color was the basic Model L of 1929 vintage. A boost in engine compression increased the LA's power, and a generator, starter, and lights modernized the tractor. This LA was photographed near Milden, Saskatchewan, Canada, on the Bailey Bros. Seeds farm.

was a two-plow machine with a smaller Waukesha engine. Heider also developed the M, a small cultivating tractor, for Rock Island in 1920. In 1925, the Heider 15/27 was introduced. Rock Island kept the Heider name on its tractors until 1928 when they were renamed Rock Island tractors, which featured a more conventional clutch and geared transmission. Rock Island discontinued tractor production in about 1935.

Massey Buys a Tractor Line

J. I. Case Threshing Machine Company became the J. I. Case Company, Inc. in 1928 after Massey-Harris purchased J. I. Case Plow Works. Begun by Case himself, the plow works was separate from Case's threshing machine company, and the two firms were often at odds with one another. Henry M. Wallis, Case's son-in-law, was president of the plow works, where he had developed the Wallis line of tractors. In 1928, Massey-Harris

bought the plow works company to get a tractor line—and in so doing became owner of the Case Plow Works name. Massey, in turn, sold the Case Plow Works name to Case Threshing Machine for a reported $700,000.

The J. I. Case Company was to undergo many more changes in the following years. In 1960, it would have been nearly impossible to imagine that Case would survive over industry leader IH in less than twenty-five years, but it would come to pass.

Case's ownership changed over the years, and, in 1967, Kern County Land Company, a majority stockholder, was bought by Tenneco of Houston, Texas. Tenneco subsequently bought IH in 1984, after the giant of the ag industry suffered massive losses due to the 1980s farm crisis. Tenneco restructured in 1988, and Case-IH became its largest division. In 1994, Tenneco spun off the Case Corporation as a new company with products identified as Case-IH machines.

1940s Case lineup
Above: *Case advertisement showing the VA, S, D, and LA Series tractors.*

1946 Case DC Wide-Front
Left: *Wide row-crop fronts were made for later-Model DCs. This 1946 model, owned by the University of California at Davis, was restored to showroom condition by the Escalon, California, Future Farmers of America chapter.*

1915 Heider C

Above: *Heider Manufacturing Company of Carroll, Iowa, built this Heider Model C in 1915. It was an improved version of the firm's first tractor, built about 1908. Friction drives transmitted power to both the pulley and the final drive. Dick Collison and Omar Langenfeld of Carroll restored this machine.*

1915 Heider C belt pulley

Right: *Infinitely variable belt pulley speeds were produced from the engine flywheel driving this friction plate. Sliding the engine forward speeded up the pulley. Levers helped the operator make speed adjustments for either pulley or forward travel.*

Heider

Burns Either Kerosene or Gasoline

Made and Sold by

Rock Island Plow Co.

Friction Transmission Means Less Gears

Less Gears Mean Less Trouble, Easier Operation and Less Cost of Upkeep

Built in Two Sizes:
Model C . . 12–20 H. P.
Model D . . 9–16 H. P.

NINE YEARS of Actual Field Work

ORIGINAL one man tractor. Burns kerosene or gasoline. First Heider sold is still in use doing good work. Heider is long past experimental stage. Special Heavy Duty, 4-cylinder, Waukesha Motor—famous Heider Friction Transmission—easy to operate—sturdy construction throughout. 7 speeds forward, 7 reverse. Two models: C 12–20 H. P. pulls three 14-inch bottoms. Model D, 9–16 H. P. pulls one plow less.

Backed by Rock Island Plow Company's 62 years' manufacturing success and reputation of Rock Island Implements all over the world. Write for the Heider's pedigree—none with better record. Catalog on request.

ROCK ISLAND PLOW CO., 525 Second Ave., ROCK ISLAND, ILL.

Also manufacturers of the famous line of Rock Island Farm Implements, including: **Tractor Plows** (no matter what tractor you use, Rock Island Tractor Plows give the best results), Discs, Drags, Plows, Planters, Seeders, Cultivators, Listers, Hay Rakes, Hay Loaders, Manure Spreaders, Cream Separators, Litter Carriers, Gasoline Engines, Stalk Cutters, Etc., Etc.

1929 Rock Island

Above: *Kin to the Heider is this 1929 Rock Island Model FA. The kerosene tractor was rated at 18/35 hp. Rim extensions gave it a wider footprint for better traction in soft conditions. Rock Island Plow Company of Moline, Illinois, was bought by Case in 1937. This tractor was restored by owner Dick Bockwoldt of Dixon, Iowa.*

Left: **1910s Heider advertisement**

Chapter 4

Caterpillar

The Monarch of the Field!
—Daniel Best ad, 1900

Above: **Caterpillar "crawler" logo**

1928 Caterpillar 2-Ton
Left: *On the same farm since new, this 1928 Caterpillar 2-Ton shows the engineering advances Caterpillar made after its first track-type tractor of 1904. Pulling on the steering bar released clutches driving each track, making the crawler turn. Individual foot-operated track brakes tightened turns. This Cat has the optional rear belt pulley.*

1890s Daniel Best steamer advertisement

Daniel Best organized the Best Manufacturing Company in 1893 to build steam- and, later, gas-engined tractors that ran on wheels or tracks. Best merged with the rival Holt crawler firm in 1908.

Tractors that "crawled" grew up in the American west, where soil conditions often called for more flotation than wheeled tractors could muster. The Holt Manufacturing Company of Stockton, California, tested its first track-type machine in 1904, when long tracks with 2-foot-wide (60-cm) wooden treads were attached to replace the rear driving wheels on a Holt steam engine. Holt and others had earlier tried to "float" their heavy machines on the soft delta soils of the San Joaquin River near Stockton. Holt attached huge wooden rim extensions on steam-engine drive wheels—sometimes 18 feet (540 cm) wide on each wheel—in an attempt to keep the monster machines from sinking into the peat soils. The endless track with wide tread worked, and the idea was adopted.

The track that contacted the ground appeared stationary and the advancing track on top appeared in motion on early moving tracks machines. One observer, photographer Charles Clements, noted, "It crawls just like a caterpillar." Holt president Benjamin Holt agreed, "Caterpillar it is. That's the name for it." Holt registered

Caterpillar as a trademark for the tracklaying machines in 1910.

Holt sold its first crawler steam tractor in 1906, and more followed. The first Holt gas-powered crawler was built about 1907. In a test by fire, Holt sold twenty-eight gas crawlers to Los Angeles for work on its massive aqueduct project. The $23 million project sought to bring water from the Sierra Nevada mountains across the Mojave Desert to the city. Working in tough conditions in desert sand, rocks, and even snow, the tractor's weaknesses showed up fast. Holt had to scurry to keep the crawlers running. Holt's "proving ground" experience on the project showed it how to build better tractors, which included all-steel construction, better spring suspensions, improved clutches, three-speed transmissions, and all-around durability.

One Holt, Two Bests, Make One Caterpillar

The Caterpillar Tractor Company was organized in 1925 by combining the assets, patents, and ideas of Holt and rival Best crawler firm. Holt bought out Daniel Best of

1920s C. L. Best 60 Tracklayer
Daniel Best's son, C. L. Best, worked with Holt for two years after the 1908 merger. But in 1910, Best formed his own company, building gas wheel and track tractors of 60 hp and 80 hp.

San Leandro, California, in 1908. Daniel Best's company, founded in 1885, was Holt's chief competitor in steam traction engines and combines, and the Holt firm looked forward to ending a bitter and contentious battle with Best.

Daniel Best's son, C. L. "Leo" Best, worked with Holt for two years after the merger, an alliance Best had opposed. In 1910, Best struck out on his own as the C. L. Best Gas Traction Company of Elmhurst, California. Gas wheel tractors of 60 hp and 80 hp were offered by the new firm, and in 1912, Best's first crawler, the Tracklayer 17-ton (15,300-kg) Model 75 was available.

With rapid growth in both model numbers and sales volume, C. L. Best's competition became a problem for Holt after World War I. During the war, Holt had concentrated on making military tractors for the government and, at the armistice, in 1918, found itself without contracts and with few farm-sized machines. At the same time, C. L. Best had concentrated on designing, building, and selling mostly farm tractors.

Although Holt was healthy financially, it was not ready for the postwar years. It needed smaller tractor designs such as Best's. For his part, Best needed more market and manufacturing facilities. So a new merger was organized, as it made sense to both parties. On March 2, 1925, C. L. Best's firm became part of the newly formed Caterpillar: it took one Holt company and two Best companies to make the Caterpillar Tractor Company.

A Hardy Holt

Holt had earlier expanded to the Midwest in 1909 to capitalize on the burgeoning need for gas farm tractors in the region. The Northern Holt Company was headquartered in Minneapolis with plans to sell tractors in the Midwest and the rapidly growing prairie provinces of Canada. By early 1910, Holt had purchased a factory in Peoria, Illinois, left vacant by the bankruptcy of the Colean Manufacturing Company. Colean had manufactured steam engines and threshing machines in the same town where the Avery Company made similar products. The Colean plant was to be the start of Caterpillar's

1925 Caterpillar Thirty
The Thirty was offered from 1925 to 1931, and was rated at Nebraska at 30.24 drawbar hp from its large four-cylinder engine. But the Thirty—like many early Cats—was a heavy machine, weighing in at 9,065 lb (4,080 kg).

midwestern expansion.

Following the organization of Caterpillar in 1925, tractor manufacture was moved to Peoria, and a subsidiary, the Western Harvester Company, was set up at Stockton to continue making combines. The combined harvester was a Holt mainstay, going back to the company's first machine of 1886. Between 1886 and 1929, Holt sold 14,111 combines. The Holt combine dominated the market in the far western wheat area and moved strongly into the Corn Belt in the mid-1920s. Combine production was moved to Peoria during the Great Depression of the 1930s. Caterpillar had tried to sell its combine business to Deere in about 1925, but Deere did not buy. Ten years later, Deere bought out the Caterpillar hillside combine and its parts inventories.

My father, John N. Sanders, Sr., was one twenty-seven-year-old midwestern farmer who believed in the

We still build round-wheel tractors for those who want them for use in favorable conditions. And no better round-wheel tractors are built anywhere.
—Daniel Best brochure, 1920s

1928 Caterpillar 2-Ton

Above: *Smallest of the Caterpillars, the 2-Ton was based on Holt designs. It was introduced in 1923 before the 1925 merger between Holt and C. L. Best. Originally gray with red lettering, this tractor, owned by Robert Garwood of Stonington, Illinois, was painted traditional Caterpillar yellow.*

1929 Caterpillar Twenty controls

Left: *The Model Twenty controls were pure Caterpillar. Small tugs on either steering clutch lever made small changes in tractor direction. Tighter turns resulted from pressure on the brake pedal while holding the same-side steering clutch. The hand clutch on the left engaged the transmission.*

1940s Caterpillar with Holt combine
A Cat D2 helped harvest soybeans on the Stonington, Illinois, farm of John N. Sanders, Sr., in the late 1940s. The Holt Combined Harvester built in Stockton, California, harvested crops for twenty-six years before it was retired in 1955. The 12-foot (360-cm) combine header was equipped with a pick-up reel to help harvest leaning and downed soybeans and wheat.

combine—especially the Holt combine. With all the optimism that youth offers, he bought a western-built Holt combine in 1929, just as soybeans started to become an important cash crop in central Illinois.

The new combine was shipped by rail from Stockton to the Wabash Railroad depot at Stonington, Illinois. There it was unloaded from the flat car and pulled 3½ miles (5.5 km) to the farm where it was set up for use. Caterpillar's dealer from Springfield, Illinois, Ralph French, sold and serviced the combine.

Pulled behind a used Deere Model D tractor, the combine soon paid for itself, custom-combining soybeans in the fall and winter wheat in the summer. A Caterpillar Model 22 tractor, followed in sequence by an R2 and then a D2, took its turn pulling the combine after the old Deere retired. Constant care and careful maintenance kept the combine in service until 1955 when it was replaced with a Case self-propelled machine.

Peoria Tractors

In 1925, the Peoria plant started turning out Caterpillar versions of the Best 30-hp and 60-hp models. Prior to the merger, Holt models included the 2-Ton (1,800-kg), 5-Ton (4,500-kg), and 10-Ton (9,000-kg). The 2-Ton was introduced in 1923 as a small state-of-the-art tractor with a Holt-made four-cylinder overhead-valve engine. After the merger, the 5-Ton and 10-Ton were dropped from the line, but the 2-Ton continued.

Caterpillar pursued the farm tractor market in the 1920s and 1930s with models ranging in power from two- up to six-plow ratings. In 1928, the Model 20 with a 20/35 rating was tested at Nebraska. In 1929, the Caterpillar 15 was announced. This gave Caterpillar five models: the 15, 20, 30, and 60; the designations roughly correlated with the machines' drawbar horsepower ratings, replacing reference to weight as before. A high-clearance version of the 10 was unveiled in 1931.

Decade of the Diesels

Caterpillar's big news in 1931 was its Diesel 65, the first diesel farm tractor offered for sale in the United States. Before Cat's pioneering work on its new diesel engine, diesels had been primarily huge marine or stationary engines. The Diesel 65 power came from a four-cylinder four-stroke engine turning at up to 650 rpm. Starting the diesel was achieved by first starting an inter-connected two-cylinder gas engine. This small, pony, engine was then clutched into the diesel engine to turn it over and get it running on its own power.

German engineer Rudolph Diesel first worked on his engine in 1892 while still a student. Within a relatively few years, thousands of stationary diesel engines hammered away in installations needing efficient, long-running power at constant loads and speeds. The diesel is typically a four-cycle engine that substitutes the heat produced in the compression stroke for a spark plug or other ignition device. Fuel is injected under pressure into the combustion chamber at the top of the compression stroke. Upon compression, the air in the cylinder is hot enough to ignite the fuel, ignition occurs, and the power stroke results. Compression ratios in diesel engines are extra high to create the heat for combustion. With the high oxygen density created by the high compression in the combustion chamber, the diesel engine is able to extract more energy from less-expensive fuels.

The diesel dilemma, just to survive the extra forces at work in the combustion chambers, is that the engines have to be heavier and stronger than gas engines of the same power size. The injection pumps that squirt the fuel into the compressed hot air in the chamber must be precisely timed, must meter fuel amounts, and must be strong enough to overcome the high compression. Add a starting device to get the engine rolling so it can "diesel" on its own, and there's another complication. Those extras all add to the cost of the machine needed to achieve the diesel's efficiency.

Caterpillar put years of research into designing its diesels, but the efforts were rewarded. By 1935, Caterpillar had made 10,000 diesel engines. Cat's fuel-efficient diesels sold tractors even though times were tough.

In 1932, Cat brought out its Model 25. In 1935, three new diesel-powered crawlers and another gas tractor were announced: the 95-drawbar-hp RD8, the 70-hp RD7, the 45-hp RD6, and the 30-hp R4 gas machine. A diesel version of the R4 came along in 1936, designated the RD4. It weighed 10,100 lb (4,500 kg), and its four-cylinder diesel turned at up to 1,400 rpm.

Cat's smallest diesel, the D2, arrived in 1938. It was designed for farm work and could pull three to four plows or a 10-foot (300-cm) disk harrow. Nebraska tests for the 7,420-lb (3,340-kg) D2 rated it at 19.4 drawbar and 27.9 belt hp. The D2's gas- and distillate-burning counterpart, the R2, was a bit lighter at 6,835 lb (3,075 kg), but it tested at a similar power output.

The D8's horsepower was increased in 1940, as was the D7's. A six-cylinder D6 debuted in 1941. The big Cat crawlers were used primarily on huge farm acreages where gang hitches of tillage or planting equipment covering wide swaths made the crawlers very efficient indeed. Western wheat growers needed the tractor's size and power at harvest to negotiate steep slopes with their big pull-type sidehill combines. Midwestern farmers gravitated toward the smaller Cats, using them for primary tillage, seed-bed preparation, and pulling heavy combines and corn pickers on thick, "gumbo" soils.

From Farming to Construction—And Back

Caterpillar led the way to diesel in the 1930s; diesel-powered farm tractors were developed by other tractor makers with increasing frequency after World War II. In 1941, Cat went off to war again, and in a sense the company didn't make it back to the farm after the war. Caterpillar bulldozers, scrapers, and other machines played a huge role in the war effort at home and in both European and Pacific theatres. The publicity Cat received for its wartime service would prove invaluable after the war as a stepping stone to increased use of the yellow machines in construction applications. Postwar, there was a lot of building to be done in the United States, and the Cats were there to do it.

Following 1930, row-crop tractors became the dominant farm tractor type. Equipping the row-crop tractors with rubber tires and adapting them with high-compression gas engines in the mid-1930s gave farmers machines with added utility. It was competition in a field that Cat seemed reluctant to rejoin until 1987 when its rubber-belted Challenger Series started crawling back to the fields to compete with four-wheel-drive rubber-tired tractors. In 1995, several versions of a row-crop rubber-belted crawler were put on the market. Only time will tell whether Caterpillar will again become a major player in the farm power arena.

1929 Caterpillar Twenty crank
Above: *A Caterpillar four-cylinder gas engine powered the Twenty. Its 1928 Nebraska test proved the 7,822-lb (3,520-kg) machine's 20/25 hp rating.*

1929 Caterpillar Twenty
Left: *New in 1928, the Caterpillar Twenty was in a series of smaller tractors aimed at the farmer. This Twenty is in the collection of Bob Feller of Gates Mills, Ohio. A Baseball Hall of Famer, Feller was known for his fastball pitches for the Cleveland Indians in the late 1940s. Feller was also a farm boy from Van Meter, Iowa, and operated a tractor just like this on his father's farm in the 1930s.*

Chapter 5

John Deere

The harder you are to please . . . the better
you'll like a John Deere.
—Deere B ad, 1949

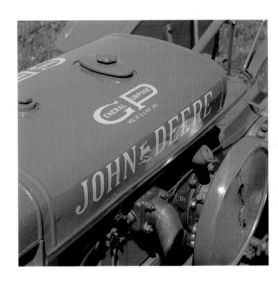

Above: **1928 Deere GP**

1934 Deere A
Left: *The new Model A of 1934 featured adjustable rear-wheel tread, hydraulic implement lift, improved brakes, and a horsepower rating of 16/23. Brass carburetors and open-shaft fans distinguished the early models. Bill Ruffner of Bellevue, Nebraska, collected this A—the 493rd one built. Model A production continued until 1952.*

Frontier blacksmith John Deere didn't give the world the steel self-scouring plow, but he did make it available.

Deere, a thirty-two-year-old blacksmith from Rutland, Vermont, made his way west to the pioneer village of Grand Detour, Illinois, in late 1836, drawn west by the promise of the frontier. Deere came with little more than his smithing tools, but he soon worked his trade mending farm equipment, wagons, stage coaches, making hand tools, and doing whatever else was needed in the small frontier town.

Grand Detour, named for its location on a loop in the Rock River, was surrounded by vast prairies of mixed tall native grasses. New settlers were just discovering that under the heavy mat of grass and prairie plants was deep, fertile soil. One exaggerated tale of the time reflected on the soil's fertility: it was said that if you stuck a crowbar into the black soil at night, it would sprout ten penny nails by morning. Previously, settlers believed that if the prairie couldn't grow trees, it couldn't grow crops.

The soil was fertile, but not easy. Breaking the sod was but the first challenge for the settlers. Keeping it cultivated was the ongoing job. That's where Deere and his products came in. His new hometown was in the midst of a sea of prairie—and a sea of opportunity.

Sticky Gumbo

Much of the sodbreaking was hired out as custom work to operators using huge (by the standards of the day) cart-mounted 16- to 24-inch (40- to 100-cm) single-bottom sodbreaking plows pulled by from four to six plodding oxen. Some farmers did their own sodbreaking with smaller plows and smaller hitches of either oxen or horses. Breaking or turning the heavy sod allowed the vegetation to deteriorate so cropping could start.

It was in the years following the sodbreaking that the new prairie farmers literally ran into a sticky problem. The heavy black gumbo soil stuck to their cast-iron plow shares and moldboards. Gummed up with sticky soil, the moldboards wouldn't turn the soil, but merely pushed it aside, coming out of the ground in the process. No matter how often the farmers scraped and scoured the bottoms with paddles or blades, the plow would gum up again just as soon as it went back into the ground. Plowing in those conditions was painfully slow, if not impossible.

Deere recognized the problem. The young blacksmith was aware of the need for a plow share and moldboard that would polish to a smooth surface and "scour" itself so the heavy soils would slide by as the plow turned

the furrow. In 1837, Deere took part of a broken steel sawmill blade, cut off the teeth with a chisel, heated it, and hammered it into a plow, then offered it for use. The steel, probably from a vertical straight "jig" type saw of the era, was already polished from its up and down strokes in Ogle County oak. The plow worked. It scoured on its own and turned over the black soil in long greasy ribbons.

The good news spread, and Deere was soon busy hammering out and polishing plows, first as a solitary venture, then with a series of partners. Deere later remembered making two plows in 1838, ten more in 1839, forty in 1840, seventy-five in 1841, and one hundred in 1842.

Plow Partners

Deere and others heard opportunity knocking. Leonard Andrus, owner of the local sawmill where Deere got his broken sawmill blade, became a partner with Deere in early 1843. That partnership operated as L. Andrus & Company. The two men built a two-story Plough Manufactory on the Rock River near Deere's blacksmith shop. They equipped it, and got serious about plowmaking.

In 1844, another partner joined them, local merchant Horace Paine. By 1846, Paine was gone, and Andrus and Deere took in Oramil C. Lathrop as a partner, operating as Andrus, Deere & Lathrop until June 22, 1847, when Lathrop apparently dropped out and the partnership was Andrus & Deere. By then the two men were making one thousand plows annually. The next year brought even more changes.

Moline Move

In May 1848, the Andrus & Deere partnership was dissolved, and Deere moved downriver near the junction of the Rock River and the Mississippi. Deere formed a new partnership in Moline, Illinois, with Robert N. Tate, an Englishman who had installed steam power for the Grand Detour plant and had worked there with Deere and Andrus. Moline, then a mere village, held more promise as a manufacturing site than Grand Detour; water power and river transportation were powerful incentives for the move.

With Tate ramrodding the venture, the Deere & Tate partnership was making plows in Moline by September 1848. John Gould, a businessman and friend of Deere's from Grand Detour, signed on as another partner that same fall, and the new Moline firm became Deere, Tate, & Gould. By 1852, the company was making 4,000 plows annually and had added a grain drill to the line. That

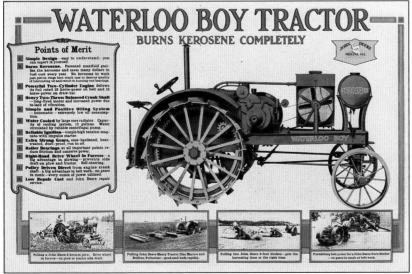

1924 Waterloo Boy N

Above: *Two forward speeds and auto-motive-type steering were features of the Waterloo Boy Model N. A Waterloo Boy 12/25 was the first tractor tested at the University of Nebraska in 1920. This 1924 N is owned by Deere fan Jim Russell of Oblong, Illinois. This Model N was the next to the last produced before Deere replaced it with the Model D.*

Left: **1920s Waterloo Boy advertisement**

1924 Waterloo Boy N

Kerosene fueled, the Waterloo Boy N kept starting gas in the small fender-mounted tanks. The guard over the bottom half of the bull gear inside the rear wheels kept dirt out to reduce gear wear. The drive wheels were originally equipped with angled cleats for field traction.

year also marked about the time the partnership members went their separate ways. Tate became a competitor in 1856, when he and Charles Buford and Buford's son, Bassett, formed a full-line plow company called Buford & Tate. That business was the basis of what later became the Rock Island Plow Co.

Meanwhile, back in Grand Detour, former Deere partner Leonard Andrus was still making plows, now with his brother-in-law, Colonel Amos Bosworth II. The Andrus firm continued with other partners and eventually became the Grand Detour Plow Company of nearby Dixon, Illinois. J. I. Case Threshing Machine Company purchased Grand Detour Plow in 1919.

John Deere is Joined by Family

Operating as "John Deere" between 1853–1857, the firm's plow production more than tripled to 13,400 units. By 1854, Deere's son, Charles, was working with the company. Following reorganizations in 1858 brought on by cash-flow problems, Charles became responsible for management. John Deere, fifty-eight at the time, remained personally involved with the firm, but apparently played a reduced role in management. Still growing in the 1860s, the company in 1863 introduced the Hawkeye sulky corn cultivator, the first Deere machine with a seat. The famous Deere-made Gilpin sulky plow of the 1870s was based on the earlier cultivator.

Deere & Company was incorporated in 1868, ending the long parade of partnerships tracing back to Grand Detour. By that time, the company was selling more than 41,000 plows, harrows, and cultivators annually. The Gilpin sulky plow was a welcome addition to the line, and by 1883, its sales—along with sales of more spring cultivators, harrows, and shovel plows—totaled nearly 100,000 units per year.

John Deere died in 1886 at the age of eighty-two, almost fifty years after he arrived in Illinois. Historians credit him with seeing values in new ideas and adapting them to his products to better serve his market and his customers. Rather than being a major inventor, Deere is considered an adapter and an imaginative marketer.

More Than Tillage Tools

Deere & Company and its branch houses attacked the next twenty-five years with more than just tillage tools, which had been its niche in its first fifty years. As the twentieth century dawned, Deere made a careful investigation of equipment and manufacturers that would complement the company's strength in tillage tools. Then it moved on its findings.

Between 1907 and 1912, Deere added the Fort Smith Wagon Company; formed John Deere Plow Company Ltd. in Canada; organized the John Deere Export Company in New York City; bought the Marseilles Manufacturing Company of Marseilles, Illinois, for its corn shellers and elevators; added Kemp & Burpee of Syracuse, New York, for its line of manure spreaders; took over the Dain Manufacturing Company of Ottumwa, Iowa, and Welland, Ontario, for its haymaking tools; picked up the Deere & Mansur corn planters, the Syracuse Chilled Plow Company, Union Malleable Iron, and Reliance Buggy Company; bought Van Brunt of Horicon, Wisconsin, for its line of grain drills; put the John Deere Wagon Works under Deere & Company; designed and built its first harvesting equipment, a grain binder, and built the Harvester Works to make the binder. It was a busy six years.

Deere assembled some of the best farm tools and their makers to become a major agricultural implement manufacturer. But the company hadn't approached the hot topic of gas traction engines, an area where its competitors were already "making smoke." Deere stayed away from steam engines and threshing machines and was apparently reluctant to enter the tractor field. But the times were changing.

Tractor Talk

Deere's branch house and dealers began to pressure the company to make a tractor. In 1912, Deere authorized the development of a tractor plow. A three-wheeled tractor plow with an undermounted three-bottom plow was created by C. H. Melvin that was similar to the Hackney Auto Plow of St. Paul.

Work on the tractor plow was stopped in 1914, and Joseph Dain, Sr., who joined Deere at the acquisition of his company, was authorized to develop a tractor for Deere with a targeted market price of $700. Dain's design was also a three-wheeler, a popular concept at the time, but the Dain machine had all-wheel drive. The first Dain was built in 1915, tested, improved, and re-tested. More test units were built and field tested in 1916 and 1917. In September 1917, Deere decided to build 100 of the Dain-designed All-Wheel-Drive Tractor.

But on March 14, 1918, before the Dains were completed, Deere bought the Waterloo Gasoline Engine Company of Waterloo, Iowa, for its famous Waterloo Boy tractor. Although the 100 Dain tractors were built, the Waterloo Boy doomed the All-Wheel-Drive design. The final price of the Dain rose to $1,700, compared with $850 for the Waterloo Boy.

Froelich Heritage

The Waterloo Gasoline Engine Company began as the Waterloo Gasoline Traction Engine Company, formed in 1893 by John Froelich and others. Thresherman Froelich constructed a gas tractor that he used successfully in his 1892 threshing season in South Dakota. Froelich mounted an upright Van Duzen single-cylinder gas engine on a Robinson steam-engine chassis and then devised gearing for propulsion. Froelich's gas traction engine could go forward and backward, and once belted to his threshing machine, it powered the machine to thresh 62,000 bushels of grain for the fifty-two-day season. Many historians consider the Froelich machine the first practical tractor. It was not, however, a commercial success.

In 1893, the new company built four more tractors, of which two were sold and returned for inadequacies. Although another tractor was built in 1896, and yet another in 1897, the young company decided to concentrate on gas engines instead. Froelich's primary interest was in the tractor, however, so he dropped out of the firm in 1895 when it was reorganized as the Waterloo Gas Engine Company.

By 1911, renewed interest in the tractor spurred more work on the machine, and by 1914, an early version of the Waterloo Boy Model R was built with an integral cylinder block for its horizontal two-cylinder engine. An opposed crankshaft set the pattern for later Deere engines. The R was soon replaced by the Model N, which featured a two-speed transmission in place of the R's one-speed. At the time of its purchase by Deere, the Waterloo company had sold more than 8,000 Waterloo Boys.

In 1920, when the University of Nebraska got its tractor tests underway, the Waterloo Boy N was the first tractor tested. The 6,183-lb (2,772-kg) machine lived up to its 12/25 rating with 12.1 drawbar and 25.51 belt hp. Its kerosene-burning engine was of 6½x7-inch (162.5x175-mm) bore and stroke. Improved versions of the N continued in production to 1924 under Deere's supervision. Among other changes, automotive-type front-wheel steering replaced the earlier fixed axle with its chain-wrap steering. In the end, about 20,000 Waterloo Boys were sold.

Deere came late to the tractor business and was in a hurry to catch up. Competition, especially from the Fordson, propelled action. During the time Deere was getting on line with the Waterloo Boy in 1918–1920, Ford sold 158,000 Fordsons. By comparison, about 13,700 Waterloo Boys were sold in the same period.

Times were tight at Deere during the economic recession after World War I; if the firm was going to stay in the tractor business, it needed an improved machine.

Birth of the Johnny Popper Legacy

Between 1919 and 1922, experimental versions of a new tractor based on the Waterloo Boy were built and tried. While most of the industry was building four-cylinder tractors, the economics of manufacture and maintenance prevailed at Deere, and the firm would produce two-cylinder tractors for the next forty years. The Model D 15/27 was the first tractor to carry the John Deere name.

The D debuted in 1923 and ran until 1953. The D was produced continuously for thirty years, the longest production run ever of a single Deere model, during which time some 160,000 units were made.

The D was a three-plow standard tractor, with an enclosed drivetrain and pressure lubrication, that could burn either kerosene or distillates. It produced 22 drawbar and 30 belt hp when tested at Nebraska in 1924. By the end of production in 1953, its power had been moved up to 38 drawbar and 42 belt hp.

Three Rows and a Lift

With the advent of IH's Farmall in 1924, Deere couldn't ignore the need for a row-crop general-purpose tractor. The Farmall was ransacking Fordson sales, and it became evident to Deere's marketing people that a tractor designed to cultivate row crops as well as pull tillage tools and run belt applications was a necessity.

Work on a three-row cultivating tractor began in 1926 and after two years of prototype testing, production started in 1928. Originally designated the Model C, the new cultivating tractor was renamed the GP for General Purpose, possibly to avoid confusion between the spoken "D" and "C" sounds. The GP was of standard four-wheel configuration with an arched front axle and drop gear housings to the rear axle to give it clearance for row-crop cultivation of three rows. The tractor straddled the center row with the front wheels and driving wheels centered between each outside row. The GP resembled the D in many respects, but the newer model was smaller and had more crop clearance.

The GP introduced, for the first time ever, a motor-driven power lift for its mounted cultivator and planter. "Power farming" had started to include operator comfort. But the GP was an early disappointment. Not all farmers were thrilled with the three-row concept, and some had trouble seeing the row when cultivating.

The result was a rush development program at Deere to remedy the GP's problems. By the cropping season of 1929, the fix was available. It was the GPWT or GP Wide Tread of tricycle design, with wide-set rear wheels and a front-mounted two-row cultivator—much like the popular Farmall. In 1931, the GP got a boost in horsepower from its original 10/20 rating up to 15/24. In 1932, the GPWT's hood was tapered at the back to aid visibility, and the steering was modified to an over-the-top configuration with improved steering characteristics.

The later-version GPWT added an adjustable cushion spring seat, spark and throttle levers mounted on the steering wheel support, and individual rear wheel brakes for shorter turns between row-pairs when planting or cultivating. Various versions of the GP were produced, including the GPO orchard version, the GP-P Series potato version, and some crawler-tracked versions assembled by Lindeman Power Equipment Company of Yakima, Washington. The GP stayed in Deere's line until 1935, although the GPWT was phased out in 1933.

Deere's Dynamic Duo

Deere's second-generation row-crop tractor was its all-time best seller. Quickening its climb up the learning

1928 Deere D

Above: *The John Deere Model D was the company's longest continually produced model; its production life ran from 1923 to 1953. With 15/27 hp, the D pulled a three-bottom plow in most soil conditions. This 1928 model has been in the same Ohio family since it was new. Deere purists think the flywheel on the D was all green when it was factory new, but owner Richard Kimball, of West Liberty, Ohio, found the flywheel rim on this D yellow, so he repainted it that way during restoration.*

Right: **1920s Deere D brochure**

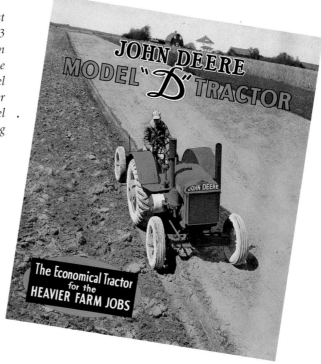

Above: **1920s Deere GP advertisement**

1928 Deere GP
Left: The first tractor with a power lift for raising attached implements, the 1928 GP (for General Purpose) was designed as a three-row, row-crop machine. An arched front axle and step-down gearing to the rear wheels gave it extra clearance for straddling the center row. The father-and-son team of James and Terry Thompson of Laurelville, Ohio, restored this gem.

> *The general-purpose type of tractor is so named because it not only does efficiently all of the things done by standard tractors, but also puts speed and economy into the planting and cultivating of row crops.*
> —John Deere's *The Operation, Care and Repair of Farm Machinery*, 1929

1933 Deere GPWT

Right: *A tricycle row-crop configuration was adopted for Deere's 1929 General-Purpose Wide-Tread. This later model, a 1933 GPWT, has the over-the-top steering, tapered hood, and adjustable spring-mounted seat first introduced in 1932. Collector-farmer Verlan Heberer of Belleville, Illinois, owns this early Deere row-crop.*

1935 Deere B

Below: *Road bands installed on this 1935 Model B made transport on paved roads lawful, as tractors with lugs were banned from many paved rural roads. The B was Deere's most popular tractor, with more than 306,000 built from 1935 to 1952. Wayne Beckom of Kokomo, Indiana, is the third generation in his family to own this B.*

curve from its GP experiences, Deere introduced the Model A in 1934. The A was a tricycle row-crop with the familiar John Deere two-lunger powerplant, but under the green and yellow paint it was all new. Infinitely adjustable rear-wheel tread, a one-piece transmission case, a hydraulic power lift that both raised and "cushion dropped" implements, centerline draft, and differential brakes geared directly to the large drive gears all made it a useful, easy handling, and efficient row-crop tractor.

The A was rated to handle two 16-inch (40-cm) plows. Nebraska tests in 1934 show 18.72 drawbar and 24.71 belt hp from its 5½x6½-inch (137.5x162.5-mm) distillate engine turning at up to 975 rpm. Production figures indicate more than 328,400 Model As in various configurations were made from 1934 to 1952. Most were the row-crop versions.

The Deere machine aimed at replacing the last team on the farm was the Model B. Advertised as being two-thirds the size of the A, the little B made 11.84 drawbar and 16.01 belt hp when first tested at Nebraska in 1934. Its 4¼x5¼-inch (106x131-mm) engine turned at up to 1,150 rpm. The B's shipping weight was 3,275 lb (1,474 kg), compared with 4,059 lb (1,826 kg) for the big-brother A. Like the A, the B also had a long and successful production run: production figures show more than 322,200 Bs made between 1935 and 1952.

Several specialized versions of the A and B were produced, including the standard-tread AR and BR, and the orchard-equipped AO and BO. Wide-row versions were designated as AW, narrow-row as AN, and Hi-Crop models as ANH and AWH. The B was also available in similar specialized versions. Starting in the early 1930s, the As and Bs were the first Deere tractors available on pneumatic rubber tires. In 1936, the orchard version of the A was streamlined to become the AO streamlined, or AOS, as today's collectors call it. More streamlining was on the way.

Dobbin and Nellie's Days are Numbered

Individual farm size increased as mechanization improved the productivity and efficiency of farmers. One farmer could do more work than ever before—and, given a larger tractor, even more. The tractor folks at Deere saw the need for a larger row-crop tractor for the large-farm market. In 1937, Deere responded with the three-plow Model G. It resembled the A and B, but the G had a stouter 6x7-inch (150x175-mm) engine tested at 20.7 drawbar and 31.44 belt hp at 975 rpm. It was heavier too. At 6,150 lb (2,768 kg), the G could pull a

10-foot (300-cm) tandem disk or easily handle four-row planters and cultivators. Available only in row-crop configurations, the G Series was in production from 1938 to 1953, and more than 60,000 were sold. Power and weight increased, and a 1947 Nebraska test of the G on rubber tires resulted in 34.49 drawbar and 38.10 belt hp output.

The year 1937 saw another tractor introduction, but on a lower end of the power spectrum. The Model 62 utility tractor was a vast departure from the other Deere models of the day. It was powered by a Deere-designed, Hercules-built vertical two-cylinder engine. Power output on the 62's tested at 7.01 drawbar and 9.27 belt hp from the 3¼x4-inch (81x199-mm) engine that revved to 1,550 rpm. The Model 62 was built as a one-plow, one-row unit for small operators including "truck farm" vegetable growers. Innovative firsts for the series included the powertrain offset to the left on the axles, with the operator's position offset to the right; this made for better forward and under-tractor visibility for careful cultivation of rowed plants. A belt pulley was available, but PTOs were not. Seventy-nine Model 62s were built in 1937 before the tractor was redesignated the Model L.

Styling or streamlining, of the L Series came in 1939. Later versions included the LA with power increased by 4 hp and rear wheels that grew from 22 inches to 24 inches (55 cm to 60 cm), and the LI industrial version painted highway yellow. Electric starting and lights were available from 1939.

Lines of the Times

By the 1930s, more and more products were being redesigned to add esthetically pleasing lines to their sometimes knobby utilitarian features. In 1937, Deere hired noted industrial designer Henry Dreyfuss and his group from New York City to help style the Model A and B tractors. Dreyfuss's work with the tractor engineers in Waterloo resulted in the streamlined and styled Models A and B introduced in 1938.

Replete with new styling, a new small row-crop, the Model H, came out in 1939. It was a handy two-row tricycle resembling the A and B, but the H was smaller with a 3½x5-inch (87.5x125-mm) two-cylinder engine turning at up to 1,400 rpm. The belt pulley on the H ran off the camshaft rather than the crankshaft as on the larger tractors; this resulted in a higher pulley location and a reversed rotation compared with the other tractors. The H's 1938 tests at Nebraska showed 12.48 drawbar and 14.84 belt hp. Deere made the H from 1939

1935 Deere B

Above: *The B was about two-thirds the size of the A and had similar features. It started on gas and was switched to kerosene or distillate when the engine was warm. Rubber tires on Kay Brunner cast-steel tractor wheels from Los Angeles, California, and rear fenders are featured on this 1935 B owned by Ken Smith of Marion, Ohio.*

Left: **1930s Deere A and B advertisement**

1936 Deere BO
Orchard growers appreciated the shielding on the Model BO (Orchard). A lowered seat and steering wheel kept the operator low to help him or her duck under tree limbs. Shields on the top kept branches from catching on fuel caps. Even the muffler was inverted to lessen damage to the trees. This 1936 BO was found and restored by Bruce Wilhelm of Avondale, Pennsylvania. His is the 350th BO made.

to 1947 in numbers exceeding 60,000. Hi-Crop versions, the HWH and HNH, were also available.

The rugged Model D got its styling facelift in 1939, and the Model G was updated to the six-speed GM in 1943. By that year, rubber tires were standard, and only rubber shortages during World War II caused a temporary return to steel wheels. Tractor model introductions were nearly curtailed at Deere during the war years as the factories and engineering departments concentrated on defense work.

Creature Comforts Become Standard
Postwar, Deere began making electric starting and lights standard equipment on its tractors. Powr-Trol for hydraulic control of pulled implements was also available from 1947. Roll-O-Matic became available on tricycle fronts to smooth out some of the front-end bumps.

Padded operator seats were a welcome addition on

Deere's new line of Model M tractors introduced in 1947. The new Dubuque, Iowa-built machine bowed as a standard-tread general-purpose utility tractor. It was the first of a new line of vertical two-cylinder-engined tractors. The M's 4x4-inch (100x100-mm) engine operated at up to 1,650 rpm, making it one of the fastest-turning engines Deere had made to that time.

The M was joined by the tricycle Model MT in 1949. Both the M and MT had Touch-O-Matic hydraulic controls for integral-mounted implements. The MT's dual system could be set to raise and lower front or rear implements separately, at the same time, or independently on the right and left sides. Power output for the M and MT was just over 14 drawbar and 18 belt hp. The M was built from 1947 to 1952, and the MT from 1949 to 1952. More than 40,500 Ms and 25,800 MTs were made.

Brother to the M and MT was the first Deere-designed and -built crawler, the MC. Deere had long supplied Model BO chassis to the Lindeman factory in Yakima, Washington. Lindeman mounted the chassis to its crawler units to make tracklayers for orchard uses in the area. In 1946, Deere acquired Lindeman and in 1949, built its own crawler based on the same vertical two-cylinder engine used in the M and MT.

The MC crawler and the MI industrial version of the M became the basis for Deere's industrial division. In 1950, Nebraska tests of the new crawler showed 18.3 drawbar and 22.2 belt hp. A credit to the MC's track design was its 4,226-lb (1,900-kg) maximum pull, compared with only 2,329 lb (1,050 kg) for the rubber-tired M. The MC came on 12-inch-wide (300-mm) tracks with 10- or 14-inch (250- or 350-mm) widths available. Tread widths available were 36 inches to 42 inches (90 cm to 105 cm). About 6,300 of the MCs were made between 1949 and 1952.

Diesel R Replaces the D

Deere's first diesel, a powerful standard-type replacement for the venerable Model D, arrived in 1949. Based on engineering and design work begun in the war years, the Model R was Deere's most powerful tractor to date. Its 5¾x8-inch (144x200-mm) diesel operated at up to 1,000 rpm and gave it 45.7 drawbar and 51 brake hp in its Nebraska test. A small electric-start two-cylinder gas starting motor put the diesel into motion. The big tractor had a shipping weight of almost 10,400 lb (4,680 kg), and showed a maximum pull of 6,600 lb (2,970 kg) in Nebraska tests. More than 21,000 of the big units were produced between 1949 and 1954.

Introduction of new models in all sizes accelerated postwar, especially in the early 1950s when tractor production had caught up with demand and tractor manufacturing and sales again became a competitive business. More horsepower and more features were the game. In the ten years from 1949 to 1959, Deere introduced six major model series.

The first of Deere's numbered tractor series was introduced in 1952. The Models 50 and 60 were worthy replacements for Deere's B and A models. New sheetmetal styling with small vertical grooves in the radiator screens gave the series a new look. Duplex carburetion with a carburetor for each cylinder helped increase performance. The PTO operated independently of the transmission or transmission clutch to provide continuous power for drawn implements. Hydraulics were also improved to live high-pressure Powr-Trol for faster lift of heavier equipment and operation independent of clutch or PTO. In 1954, industry firsts for the series included factory-installed, optional power steering and rack-and-pinion adjustment of the rear wheel tread.

The 70 joined the numbered series in 1954 as the replacement for the G. The 70 was offered in gasoline, "all fuel," or LPG versions, as were the 50 and 60. In 1954, the 70 was available with a diesel engine as Deere's first diesel row-crop tractor. Drawbar and brake hp tests at Nebraska resulted in 20.62/26.32 for the 50, 27.71/35.33 for the 60, 42.24/48.29 for the gas 70, and 34.25/43.77 for the diesel 70. Several different front- and rear-axle versions were available as were Hi-Crop models for those growers needing high-clearance capabilities. The 60 and 70 were also made as standard-tread models, and the 60 was available as an orchard tractor. More than 33,000 of the 50 and 64,000 of the various 60 models were made from 1952–1956, and 43,000 of the 70 were manufactured from 1953 to 1956.

Upgraded versions of the Dubuque-made M were introduced in 1953 as numbered models. They were the 40 standard, 40 tricycle, and 40 crawler. The 40s also wore the new grill treatment of the 50, 60, and 70 models. Improved hydraulics and other systems were similar to those on the larger tractors. Power was increased on the 40s by about 15 percent compared with the earlier Ms. The new 40 crawler sported four or five track rollers, depending on track length. The 40 Series was produced between 1953 and 1955.

Meeting the demand for more horsepower in its largest tractor, Deere replaced the R with the diesel Model 80 in 1955. The big 80 showed 46.32 drawbar and 57.49 belt hp. It was also upgraded to include the same hydraulic systems and live PTO as the other numbered models had. The R was produced from 1955 to 1956, when it was upgraded to a new model designation.

The two-tone 20 Series arrived in 1956. In addition to yellow on the wheels, the 20s had a yellow stripe on the hood bottom continuing down the sides of the radiator shroud. The Waterloo-made tractors—the 520, 620, and 720—had new engines featuring improved cylinder heads and pistons to increase combustion-chamber turbulence for more output and fuel efficiency. The Dubuque-made tractors included a smaller version, the 320, rated as a one-to-two-plow tractor with the hydraulics of the other models. The 420 superceded the 40 Series and was made in tricycle, standard, Hi-Crop, utility, wide-tread, low-profile, and crawler versions. The 820 diesel replaced the 80 as the big gun in the line. After a power increase, the 820 pulled 52.5 drawbar and 64.26 belt hp in its 1957 Nebraska test.

1937 Deere AOS

Above: *Designed to cruise carefully through orchards and groves without damage to crops, this 1938 Model AO qualifies as being streamlined before the other Deere tractors got their facelifts. Additional side shields were available for citrus operations. Fans refer to this model as AOS (for AO Streamlined). Deere collector Edwin Brenner of Kensington, Ohio, and his father restored this tractor in 1984.*

1937 Deere AOS

Left: *The operator sat low and well back on the AOS. The steering wheel was mounted below the operator shield to keep it from catching limbs and branches.*

They're Tomorrow's Tractors Today.
—Deere A and B ad, 1938

Last of the Johnny Poppers

The world could not know, but the 30 Series tractors introduced in 1958 were to become the last of Deere's two-cylinder tractors. Operator comfort and ease of use were hallmarks of the series. A new deep-cushioned seat positioned the operator between two new flat-top fenders with built in dual lights. A new dash design tilted the engine instruments for better visibility. The steering-wheel column emerged from the dash, positioning the wheel on an angle for more comfortable steering. The Dubuque tractors, still using the vertical two-cylinder engines, were the 330 and the 430 in many tread and axle configurations, and the crawler 430.

From the Waterloo tractor plant came the 530, 630, 730, and 830 models and their derivatives. Engine starting on the 730 diesel was changed over to electric start, eliminating the gas-starting engine. The last two-cylinder model introduced by Deere was the Model 435 diesel powered with a General Motors engine. The 435 diesel was the first Deere tractor tested at Nebraska that received a PTO horsepower rating rather than a belt horsepower rating.

Shades of things to come coincided with the surprise introduction in fall 1959 of a monster four-wheel-drive

1937 Deere 62

Above: *Only seventy-eight of the cute 1937 Model 62s were made before the tractors became the unstyled Model Ls. The 62, a small utility tractor, had a vertical two-cylinder engine running up to 1,500 rpm for a 7/9 hp rating. Unlike other Deere tractors, the Model 62 and the following Model L had foot clutches instead of hand clutches. Ronald Jungmeyer of Russellville, Missouri, restored his Model 62, the 48th made.*

1938 Deere G

Facing page, top: *Considered a large three-plow tractor when it came out in 1937, the Model G boasted 20/31 hp and was the most powerful tractor Deere made up to that time. A PTO was standard on the model. This 1938 G was found and restored by Lloyd Simpson of Monroe, North Carolina. Serial number is #2132.*

1939 Deere BR

Facing page, bottom: *Owner Robert Waits completely rebuilt and restored this once worn-out 1939 Model BR, serial #330533. The Rushville, Indiana, farmer says the standard-tread B was shipped to Yorkton, Saskatchewan, Canada, from the Waterloo, Iowa, factory shortly after it was built. Model BRs were built from 1936 to 1947, but in much fewer numbers than the row-crop Model B.*

1939 Deere H

Styled from its start in 1939, the new Model H carried the lines of the Henry Dreyfuss-styled Models A and B introduced the year before. Similar in most ways to its larger siblings, the H was a smaller machine rated at 9.68/12.97 hp. Its forte was cultivating and other light jobs where its small size and ease of handling were desired. Leonard Bruner of Rising City, Nebraska, spent more than 300 hours restoring this tractor, serial #4140.

8010 with a company rating of 150 drawbar hp from a 215-hp engine. It could pull a mounted eight-bottom plow at 7 mph (11 km/h), lift the plow at the row end, and turn sharply back into the next furrow. Articulated power steering with air brakes aided its control. Another version, the 8020, came out in 1960 to add an eight-speed Syncro-Range transmission, oil-cooled clutch, and other improvements. Somewhat ahead of its time, neither version sold well.

New Generation of Power

On August 30, 1959, the world learned what the Deere engineers had been doing for the past six years. That date marked the unveiling to Deere dealers of the New Generation of Power tractors in Dallas, Texas. The 1010, 2010, 3010, and 4010 were all new from front to back. Proven Deere concepts like weight concentrated on the rear wheels was achieved by keeping the engines to the

rear, close to the transmission and differential. Up front were the large-capacity fuel tank and radiator. And, powering the new machines were all-new vertical, four- and six-cylinder engines. There was not a two-cylinder engine in the line.

The four-cylinder 3010 and the six-cylinder 4010 were available as diesels, as well as gas or LPG versions. High horsepower-to-weight ratios gave the new line of tractors the advantages of higher operating speeds and a smaller percent of power needed to move the tractor; that added efficiency to the new line's obvious advantages of increased power. The 4010 produced 73.65 drawbar hp, but weighed less than 7,000 lb (3,150 kg). The 3010 diesel pulled more than 50 drawbar hp and was a full four-plow tractor.

Added to the other firsts, the new series provided closed-center hydraulics for live implement-raising muscle in three circuits. Power steering and power brak-

1953 Deere R

The diesel-powered Model R of 1949 was a big, husky replacement for the venerable Model D. The utility gasoline pony engine was used for starting the 416-ci (6814-cc) diesel engine. Turning at up to 1,000 rpm, the two-cylinder diesel gave the tractor 34.27/43.32 hp at Nebraska. The R was Deere's first diesel and its first tractor of more than 40 hp. This restored 1953 R works at tractor pulls in Missouri and Iowa. Owner David Walker of Chillicothe, Missouri, found this tractor in the wheat fields of eastern Colorado, brought it home, and put it back into like-new condition.

ing were also served by the new variable-displacement pump working from a common reservoir of hydraulic fluid. New eight-speed Syncro-Range transmissions matched power and speed to job demands.

Other power sizes in the series were the 1010 with 30 drawbar hp and the 2010 with 40 drawbar hp. The 1010 was of utility configuration, but with adjustable front and rear tread to handle row-crop work. The 2010 was offered in tricycle row-crop or row-crop utility versions.

The years following the introduction of the new line proved the wisdom of Deere's gamble. Farmer acceptance was outstanding, and Deere's share of the U.S. wheel tractor market shot up from 23 percent in 1959 to 34 percent in 1964. By 1963, Deere had outpaced rival IH to become the number one farm and light industrial equipment manufacturer. At present, Deere has maintained that leading position for thirty years.

Now—a Tractor that will Replace Your Animal Power.
—Deere H ad, 1939

1954 Deere 60

Above: *The Models A and B were replaced with the first numbered series starting in 1952. This 60 is a standard-tread version based on the row-crop tractor with its adjustable rear axles and high seat placement. The series offered gas, all-fuel, and LPG engines, as on this tractor equipped for rice-field work. Owner Ford Baldwin of Lonoke, Arkansas, collects Deere rice models.*

1959 Deere 630 Hi-Crop

Right: *Specialized versions of Deere tractors were widely used. This 1959 630 Hi-Crop was first sold and used for growing vegetable crops in Florida. The model's 32-inch (80-cm) clearance let it work in staked tomatoes and other high-growing row crops. Owners Ron Coy and Gerald Holmes of New Richland, Minnesota, resurrected their rare all-fuel Hi-Crop (serial #6312292) from little more than rusting metal found in eastern Florida.*

1959 Deere 530

Adjustable wide-front axles were popular options on the 530 tractors introduced in 1958. The 30 Series marked the last of Deere's long tradition of two-cylinder tractors. This Model 530 is owned by Ken Smith of Marion, Ohio.

1959 Deere 3010 and 4010

The New Generation of Power tractors introduced by Deere in the summer of 1959 are represented by these immaculately restored 3010 and 4010 diesels. Owned by farmer-collector Ken Smith of Marion, Ohio, each tractor wears serial number #1000, indicating they were the first machines manufactured in 1961. The landmark series helped move Deere to its present spot as the number-one maker of farm equipment.

Chapter 6

Ford

Henry Ford's presence in the implement province and the new type of competition he soon introduced returned the industry for a time to the atmosphere of battle.
—Cyrus McCormick III
The Century of the Reaper, 1922

Above: **1939 Ford-Ferguson 9N**

1923 Fordson
Left: *Detroit auto magnate Henry Ford dominated the American tractor market for nearly a decade with his Fordson tractor, introduced in 1917. The Fordson popularized farm tractors by providing a small, affordable, serviceable machine. The Fordson's price dropped to $395 during tractor price wars after World War I. This Fordson is like the one used by owner Robert Mashburn's father when Robert was a small boy. The Bolton, Mississippi, soybean and cotton farmer restored this 1923 model.*

Henry Ford and his company had a huge impact on tractor design and manufacturing in the United States. This influence came in two major thrusts: first with the Fordson of 1917; and then with the landmark Ford-Ferguson of 1939. Although separated by more than twenty years, both tractors were milestone machines that drastically changed the way tractors were made and used.

Henry Ford, like many Americans of his era, was a farm boy. He was born near Dearborn, Michigan, in 1863, and as a boy and young man had hands-on experience with farm work on his father William Ford's farm. Ford's experience with horses propelled him to mechanize work he considered drudgery. He first began to experiment with steam engines while still on the farm. In 1893, while employed as an engineer with the Edison Illuminating Company in Detroit, his efforts turned to internal-combustion engines. In his spare time, Ford made his first automobile.

By 1903, Ford had organized the Ford Motor Company. In 1908, his company started mass-producing the famous Model T automobile—a simple, inexpensive, and highly popular car that put America on wheels. By the end of its production run in 1927, the Tin Lizzie had rolled off the Ford assembly lines in a record run of 15 million copies.

Ford built an experimental Automobile Plow in 1907 using one of his 1903 Model B car engines and transmission. More experimental tractors followed, and in 1915, Ford announced he would build a light two-plow tractor to sell for $200. Other entrepreneurs were listening. Seeing gold in the name Ford, a Minneapolis group quickly organized the Ford Tractor Company in 1916, using the name of participant Paul B. Ford. The Minneapolis firm began to produce a tractor it called the Ford tractor, hoping Henry Ford would pay to use the name on his own machine. Few of the awkward Minneapolis machines were made, but their presence caused Henry Ford to organize his tractor company in 1917 as Henry Ford & Son and to name his tractor the Fordson; Ford's son was Edsel.

The Detroit Growler

The 1917 Fordson was unconventional in the era of heavy two-cylinder tractors and odd three-wheel designs. Although the Fordson looks fairly conventional in hindsight today, with its standard-wheel configuration of large drive wheels in the rear and smaller automotive-type steering gear in the front, it was viewed as strange at the time. The Fordson was equipped with a

1920s Fordson advertisement

four-cylinder 4x5-inch (100x125-mm) inline gas engine mounted lengthwise. Its 1,000-rpm 20-hp engine used Ford's Model T ignition with a flywheel-mounted dynamo supplying current to a vibrating high-tension coil on the engine block. The engine castings bolted to the transmission housing, producing a frameless unit, was one of the first of its type.

The Fordson's multiple-disk clutch ran in oil, whereas splash engine lubrication was augmented with oil circulated by use of funnel and trays to distribute oil through the engine. Final drive from the transmission was through a worm gear in the enclosed differential housing to the enclosed axles then out to the rear drive wheels. The Fordson weighed about 2,700 lb (1,215 kg). Its three-speed transmission gave it speeds of up to 6.8 mph (10.8 km/h) in third gear, and it could plow at 3 mph (4.8 km/h). The little rig was considered a two-plow tractor.

The Ford mystique among farmers, due to the success of the Model T car, and the tractor's price of $750 when domestic production started in spring of 1918, put the little machine in business. Although more expensive than Ford predicted in 1915, the tractor took off

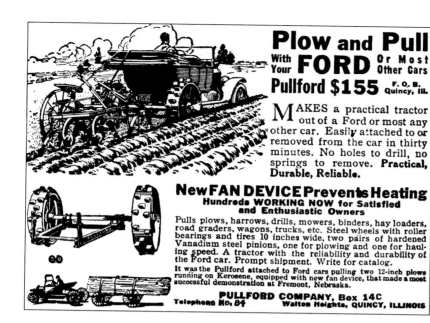

1910s Ford Automobile Tractor
Numerous firms across the United States offered conversion kits to turn the ubiquitious Ford Model T automobile into a farm tractor, including the Pullford Company of Quincy, Illinois. These kits ranged from rear-end conversions to full row-crop tractor makeovers.

with immediate sales to 34,167 in 1918, 57,000 in 1919, and 67,000 in 1920. By 1922, Fordson sales were up to 69,000 and accounted for 70 percent of all U.S. tractors sold; in 1923, the Fordson share shot to nearly 102,000 units for 76 percent of all gas tractors sold in the country. That was the same year Deere's Model D was announced, and one year before IH's Farmall hit the market.

Tractor Wars

By 1921, the United States was in a post-World War I recession, and Fordson sales were down by 45 percent to only 36,793 tractors. Ford responded by cutting the price of the tractor in three different price reductions to a low of $395. His competitors also cut prices, and a price war was on.

The farm implement leader of the day, IH not only cut prices for its 10/20 Titan to $700, but threw in a free plow. IH also took the ultimate competitive action of developing a better product, a general-purpose tractor that would eclipse Ford and other makers in its all-around farming utility. The new IH tractor was introduced in 1924 as the row-crop Farmall, another seminal tractor that, like the Fordson, moved farm mechanization a giant step ahead.

The Fordson lost market share to the Farmall, as did most other tractors. By 1928, IH was back in the lead with 47 percent of the U.S. tractor market, and in 1929, IH made 60 percent of the tractor sales in the country. Ford sales plunged; the firm decided to stop making the Fordson in the United States in 1928 and moved pro-

duction to Cork, Ireland. Almost 740,000 American-made Fordsons had been built from 1917 to 1928.

The Irish-made Fordsons were improved with a larger-displacement engine equipped with a high-tension magneto. Fenders and a new wheel design distinguished the Irish-made Fordsons from the domestic models. A water pump was finally added to help engine cooling. Many of the Irish Fordsons were imported into North America.

In 1933, Fordson production was shifted to Dagenham, England, where it continued until 1938. The first Fordson row-crop tractor, the tricycle All Around, was introduced in 1937 by the English Ford Motor Company, Ltd. By the end of Fordson production in England in 1938, another wave of Ford's ingenuity was about to wash over the United States. This time Ford had help from abroad, an Irish inventor named Harry Ferguson.

Gentleman's Agreement Gives Farmers a Lift

Both Henry Ford and inventor Harry Ferguson long dreamed of making implements integral to the tractor, avoiding the tacked-on way of hitching implements. That practice had carried forward to tractors after they nearly replaced the horse. Many farmers modified their horsedrawn equipment for tractor use simply by sawing off the long wooden tongue and attaching a new strap iron hitch.

Ferguson worked on his integral hitch dream for years and made it a working reality. He demonstrated his Ferguson System to Ford at Ford's Fairlawn, Michigan, farm in fall 1938. Ferguson's tractor with its integral three-point hydraulically controlled hitch worked well. Models of the system helped visually explain how it all worked. Ford was impressed and wanted to buy Ferguson's patents on the spot. Ferguson indicated they were not for sale at any price. So the two men made an oral agreement, not committed to paper or witnessed by others, just sealed with a handshake.

According to Ferguson's later recollection, the agreement stated that Ferguson would be in charge of design and engineering; Ford would build the tractor and assume those inherent risks; Ferguson would distribute the tractors wherever and however he pleased; and either party could end the agreement at any time for any reason. Then the men went to work.

In June 1939, they were ready. The Ford Model 9N tractor with Ferguson System boasted a 120-ci (1966-cc) four-cylinder high-compression gas engine of 3³⁄₁₆x3³⁄₄-inch (79x94-mm) bore and stroke. The engine's pistons, rings, valves, and connecting rods were the same as those in Ford's 1939 Mercury V-8. Ford rated it at 28 hp at 2,000 rpm; Nebraska tests in 1940 showed 16.31 drawbar and 23.56 belt hp. It managed a pull of 2,146 lb (966 kg).

Of standard wheel configuration, the Ford's front axle was adjustable in width, and the rear wheels could be reversed on dished rims so the tractor would straddle two rows. Rubber tires were standard as was the generator and starter. Also standard was the PTO and the Ferguson System of hydraulics for control and lift of three-point mounted implements. The 9N even came with a muffler in the under-mounted exhaust system. Only the electric lights and rear-mounted two-bottom plow and row-crop cultivator were optional.

The Ford-Ferguson, as it came to be known, was a thoroughly modern tractor, from its streamlined radiator grill to its three-point hitch on the business end. It was not in any sense just a re-do of the old Fordson. Comfortably straddling the transmission housing, the operator sat forward of the rear wheels for a smoother ride. To the driver's right was a small lever controlling the hydraulics. Stops were provided on the lever guide for implement depth settings. Operating the tractor was so easy that a child could do it—and many did.

Two trailing lift arms hinged from the bottom of the axle were linked to the built-in hydraulic lift arms on the upper part of the transmission. The third point of implement attachment was to a high-mounted centered link working in concert with the lift arms. Ferguson's integral hitch worked as if the three points of implement attachment converged near the center of the tractor's front axle. That let the implement trail, as if it were attached at the front axle center.

The 9N's new concepts led other manufacturers to imitate and improve on its features for the next twenty years. The Ferguson System started a revolution, and all tractor and equipment design thereafter was influenced by—if not a direct copy of—Ferguson's genuis.

Sales of the handy little tractor were brisk. By the end of 1940, more than 35,000 9Ns had been built, and in 1941, another 43,000 had come off the production line. That all changed abruptly in 1942 as war efforts shifted production to other products and tractor production was severely limited. Postwar production resumed at a brisk pace: between June 1939 and July 1947, more than 300,000 Model 9N and 2N Ford-Fegusons were built.

The Model 2N had been introduced in late 1942. It included improvements that helped the operator and added to safety. The left brake pedal was moved to the right side with the right brake pedal so an operator could disengage the clutch with the left foot while braking both rear wheels with the right foot. On the 9N, the left wheel brake and clutch pedals were both on the left, making it impossible to operate the left brake and the clutch simultaneously, as might be needed when stopping and turning at a field's end. The 2N also included a lockout on the starter that prevented operation if the transmission was in gear. Other changes included the elimina-

1928 Fordson on Trackson
Facing page, top: *Fordsons came from Detroit, Michigan, without options—a situation soon remedied by many other companies. This track conversion made in Milwaukee, Wisconsin, is the Trackson Full Crawler unit. Its differential steering works through the large brakes on the drive sprockets. Steer left, the left track is braked and the right one speeds up; steer right and the opposite happens. Richard Stout of Washington, Iowa, found and restored this converted 1928 Fordson.*

1929 Irish Fordson
Facing page, bottom: *Major improvements marked the Fordsons imported from Ireland after Ford shifted production to Ireland in 1928. More power, rear fenders with built-in toolboxes, new wheels, and a high-tension magneto made this 1929 Irish Fordson a safer, easier-to-start, better-performing tractor than its earlier, American-made versions. James Hostetler of West Liberty, Ohio, found his tractor near home and restored it with his family's help.*

tion of chrome trim on the tractor. Due to rubber rationing during the war, some 2Ns were supplied with steel wheels.

The Handshake Agreement Fails

Postwar recovery put stresses on tractor manufacturers to make up for lost time and meet the heavy demand for machines. War price controls had resulted in massive losses on the Ford tractor. No price increases were allowed during the war so Ford must have felt those pressures in 1946 when the company tried to renegotiate its agreement with Ferguson to either buy him out or buy into his distribution rights. The parties could not come to terms, and the 1938 Gentleman's Agreement was ended effective December 31, 1946. Ford-Ferguson was no more, but Ford agreed to make tractors for Ferguson to sell through June 1947.

Ford quickly established its own distribution firm, Dearborn Motor Corp. Just as Ford ended production for Ferguson in June 1947, Ford also announced its own Model 8N tractor. The 8N was not much different than the Ford-Ferguson 2N, except for its colors and some improvements. The tractor engine, drivetrain, and axles were red, and the hood, fenders, and wheel rims were a warm gray. Ford's red-painted script trademark was stamped into the fenders and hood. The 8N had a four-speed constant-mesh transmission, better brakes and steering gear, and an improved starter lockout. And it had the same hydraulic three-point hitch and implement control sysem as before. Patent infringement? Royalties? No payments were made, so Ferguson sued Ford for $251 million, claiming infringement and damages that impacted his business.

Ferguson was meanwhile busy on the manufacturing front too, going it alone in the tractor business. His 2N look-alike was the TE-20, assembled in Coventry, England. Soon after introduction of the TE-20, the Model TO-20 was built in Detroit at a daily rate of one hundred units.

The Ferguson lawsuit dragged out for four years, and when it was finally resolved, a worn-down Ferguson settled for only $9.25 million. Some of the Ferguson patents had expired by that time, so Ford had to redesign only a few of its parts to continue producing tractors with the hydraulically controlled three-point system of implement control.

Fords for the Future

To mark the Ford Motor Company's fiftieth, golden anniversary in 1953 of its 1903 founding, Ford brought out the Model NAA Jubilee. It came with Ford's first valve-in-head tractor engine. The new Red Tiger engine had a displacement of 134 ci (2195 cc) and turned out 31.14 hp at 2,000 rpm to give the Jubilee power to pull three plows. A new grill design and treatment distinguished it from the 8N. Just slightly taller and longer than the 8N, the Jubilee was produced only between 1953 and 1955.

In 1955, Ford branched out, debuting five new models in two power sizes. The three-plow 600 Series and four-plow 800 Series were available in gas and LPG versions.

In 1958, the first Ford tractors with American-made diesels were the Models 801 and 901. By 1959, the Powermaster and Workmaster Series arrived with a choice of gas, diesel, or LPG engines. In 1961, the push for power led Ford to introduce its largest tractor to date, the five-plow six-cylinder diesel Model 6000 producing 66 hp.

By the time of Henry Ford's death in 1947, some 1.7 million tractors bearing his name had come forth from Ford factories. Mass-production techniques, including Ford's famed assembly line, taught the world how to make tractors. Vast changes in the intervening years since Henry Ford's death have further altered tractor design and changed where and by whom they are made.

In 1985, Ford combined its tractor operations with New Holland by buying the company from the Sperry Corporation. Ford New Holland was sold by Ford to the Fiat Group of Italy in 1990. The familiar Ford oval trademark with the script name has disappeared from tractors; block letters spelling Ford can be used only until 2001 under agreement with Fiat. The company selling "Ford" tractors in 1995 was New Holland, Inc., the new name of the Fiat-owned firm.

1938 English Fordson N

Above: *Among the later Fordsons is this imported 1938 English-built Fordson N, rebuilt and redone in its original orange paint by Richard Vogt of Enid, Oklahoma. Fordson production moved from Cork, Ireland, to Dagenham, England, in 1933. In 1938, the Fordson All-Around tricycle row-crop tractor was introduced. It, too, was imported into North America, but in relatively small numbers.*

Right: **1950s Ford Golden Jubilee advertisement**

1939 Ford 9N

Above: *Harry Ferguson's contribution to the 9N was its three-point hitch linked to a built-in hydraulic system. It provided draft-sensing that supplied both up and down pressure to the implement. Freeman Miles' tractor mounts the two-bottom plow that became an integral part of the machine once attached to the three-point hitch.*

1939 Ford 9N

Left: *More revolutionary on the inside than the outside, the 1939 Ford-Ferguson 9N blazed new trails in implement mounting and control with its hydraulically controlled integral hitch. Long-time Ford tractor dealer Freeman Miles of Dothan, Alabama, sold this 1939 9N new for $575, the first 9N sold in Alabama. Rubber tires, electric starting, and PTO were standard, but lights were extra. Miles later took this 9N as a trade on a newer tractor. He rebuilt it, and kept it for display.*

> *To Lift the burden of farming from flesh and blood and place it on steel and motors.*
> —Henry Ford

Chapter 7

International Harvester

"It is hard for a young farmer like me to realize there ever was a time when there was no Farmall System of Farming."
—IH Farmall ad, 1941

Above: **1941 Farmall MD**

1928 Farmall Regular

Left: *The row-crop tractor concept began with the McCormick-Deering Farmall, first offered in 1924. It changed the way tractors were made and used—and even chased most horses from the farm. This 1928 model shows the open-gear steering that marked the model. In addition to its versatility in cultivating row crops and handling tillage chores, the 1928 model also offered both belt pulley and PTO power for other farm power needs. Robert Lessen of Hartsburg, Illinois, restored this tractor.*

The beginnings of the International Harvester Company trace back to 1831 and Rockbridge County, Virginia, where Cyrus Hall McCormick first crafted a successful grain reaper. Improving on ideas tried earlier by his father Robert McCormick, Jr., young Cyrus, at twenty-two, showed his machine to the public in 1831. By 1834, McCormick held a patent on his ideas, and by 1840, had sold his first machine.

The reaper was a major step in revolutionizing grain harvest. It eliminated the back-wrenching human toil of swinging a scythe or cradle to cut grain. McCormick's reaper could cut three times as much wheat in a day as a good worker with a scythe. Later on, binders could cut and bind seventeen times as much wheat in a day as a farm worker. When coupled with the new threshing machines, human productivity was multiplied many times and food production soared.

Like other farm machine developments of the day, McCormick's reaper had lots of company—other inventors and makers pursuing the goal of the perfect harvester. Some of these inventors' and makers' efforts would later shape the way grain was harvested, as well as form the companies that would later make the harvest equipment.

Leading the Revolution

Once proven successful in Virginia, McCormick headed west with his reaper in 1847 for the promise of larger markets in the awakening prairies. Like other pioneering farm equipment makers, such as John Deere and J. I. Case who moved to the west during that era, McCormick's pick of geography and timing were just right. McCormick built his reaper plant in Chicago, a location that was later to become home to the huge International Harvester.

Reapers began to flow from the plant, with some 4,000 marketed between 1848 and 1850; up to 1848, only about 1,200 reapers had been built. Cyrus' brothers, Leander and William S., soon joined him in the business and played roles in its success. With the continuing popularity of the reaper, all three prospered. William died in 1865, and in 1879, the partnership was incorporated as McCormick Harvesting Machine Company. Cyrus died in 1884, and in 1890, his widow, Nancy, and son, Cyrus, Jr., bought out Leander's shares. Cyrus, Jr. was to successfully lead the company for many years after his father's death.

The 1871 Chicago fire destroyed the plant and left the firm with a $600,000 loss. Vital records, fortunately, were recovered intact. The factory was replaced in 1872–

1873 on a new, larger site as a bigger, more modern plant.

By buying patents that showed promise, and innovating, and negotiating manufacturing rights from others, McCormick Harvesting Machine Company was able to keep up with the fierce competition from rival firms. But there was one aggressive manufacturer bearing down on the company right there in Chicago.

In 1870, William Deering, originally a well-off dry-goods wholesaler from Maine, invested in an Illinois reaper called the Marsh harvester and helped it to develop and succeed. It was originated by brothers Charles W. and William W. Marsh of Shabbona Grove, Illinois, and was first patented in 1858. The Marsh machine was a forerunner of the binder.

By 1880, Deering had become the sole owner of the Deering Harvester Company. At that time, he sold twine-tie binders combining the strengths of the Marsh harvester with those of the Appleby twine binder. Within the next decade, the McCormick and Deering firms were both on top as harvester providers and were beginning to compete for sales of related harvesting equipment. Deering tried to sell out to McCormick in 1897, but financing couldn't be arranged. Both firms had strained themselves financially trying to keep up with the other.

IH Conceived in New York

A merger plan for McCormick and Deering was worked out in 1902 in the New York offices of J. P. Morgan. It was a plan that solved McCormick and Deering's competitive dilemma. The new International Harvester was formed by combining the assets of McCormick Harvesting Machine, Deering Harvester, Plano Manufacturing Company of Plano, Illinois, Milwaukee Harvester Company of Milwaukee, and Champion Reaper Works. The new company was huge for the times, with a $120 million capitalization.

IH soon combined the best features of the harvesting equipment it had acquired and moved forward into the twentieth century to capture other markets. Its foreign trade grew rapidly in Europe, the British Empire, South America, Africa, and Russia. A new factory was built in Hamilton, Ontario. New equipment lines were added by buying their manufacturers. In 1903, the old rival D. M. Osborne Company was bought. The Weber Wagon Company of Chicago was added. Next came Aultman-Miller of Akron, Ohio. Tillage, haying, and other lines came with the purchase of the Keystone Company of Rock Falls, Illinois, in 1904. IH's first European plant was built at Norrkoping, Sweden, in 1905. Other plants in Germany, France, and Russia fol-

1917 International Harvester Mogul 10/20

Above: *IH already had eight years of tractor-making experience when it announced its 8/16 Mogul in 1914. It was a popular tractor that spawned the more powerful 10/20 Mogul in 1916. The Mogul's belt pulley ran next to the flywheel and was clutched into motion with the small hand wheel inside its central protective shield. Brothers Howard and Roger Schnell of Franklin Grove, Illinois, restored their father's 1917 machine in 1989.*

1917 International Harvester Mogul 10/20 starting procedure

Right: *Team effort from the Schnells brought the Mogul's one-cylinder engine to life. The one-lunger tractor sold by IH's McCormick dealers had to compete with the two-cylinder Titan 10/20 sold by the company's Deering dealers. Titans sold nearly nine-to-one over the one-lunger sales, thus ending the IH single-cylinder era.*

Mogul & Titan tractors are the best on the market to-day because quality and design have not been sacrificed for price.
—IH ad, 1920s

lowed. International was international. These were boom years for IH, but more was to come.

Time for Tractors

A powerful rhythmic pounding sound was starting to echo over the prairies, the noise of the newfangled gas traction engine. IH heard it as another opportunity and responded with a machine of its own—or at least partly its own. In 1906, IH put one of its horizontal single-cylinder 15-hp Famous gas engines made at the Milwaukee Works onto a Morton-made friction-drive truck, or chassis. It worked, so IH made more of its Type A tractor that year for testing, and another 200 in 1907.

The Type A's friction drive soon gave way to gears, except for a friction-drive reverse. More than 600 Type As with 12-, 15-, or 20-hp engines were made between 1907 and 1911. A Type B with a 20-hp engine and a full-length rear axle was offered, but only 301 were made. By 1909–1912, a two-speed Type A with 12 hp was available, but only sixty-five were built. Although sales figures were modest by any measure, IH was already leading the industry in 1911 in sales of gas traction engines.

IH had kept separate dealerships from its 1902 merger and tried to give them different tractors to sell. The Mogul and Titan names were chosen for the two tractor lines with Moguls made for McCormick dealers and Titans for Deering dealers. Tractor production was added at the Chicago plant in 1910, the year the 45-hp Mogul came out. The Mogul was powered by a two-cylinder horizontally opposed engine rated at 345 rpm. In 1911, a larger, but similar Mogul 30/60 was introduced. The 1911 two-cylinder Titan was also made first as a 45-hp tractor, then upgraded to 30/60 rating with a larger engine.

In 1912, a 15/30 Mogul went into production. It was a one-cylinder version of the 30/60. The 15/30 engine turned at 400 rpm. The 1913 Mogul was rated at 12/25 hp from a two-cylinder horizontally opposed engine. The models were heavy monsters, and looked more like steam engines than gas tractors.

IH's First Four and New Lightweights

A Titan with a four-cylinder (or double twin) horizontal crossmount engine joined the IH line in 1914. Begun as a 12/25, the Titan was upgraded to 15/30 by 1918. It was a four-plow tractor weighing 8,700 lb (3,915 kg). It had a two-speed spur-gear transmission that gave it operating speeds of 1.9 and 2.4 mph (3 and 3.8 km/h) at an engine speed of 575 rpm. Heavy roller chains transmitted power to the 5-foot-diameter (150-cm) rear

wheels. It sported a cell-type front-mounted radiator cooled with a belt-driven fan. Many were equipped with an enclosed cab. The 15/30 was manufactured in Milwaukee between 1915 and 1922, and its various versions sold about 5,500 copies.

The most popular of the IH tractors to date came in 1914. It was the lighter-weight two-plow Mogul 8/16. The 8/16 had a one-cylinder 8x12-inch (200x300-mm) 400-rpm horizontal engine with hopper cooling. It had one-speed forward, for 2 mph (3.2 km/h), and reverse. Narrow spacing of the two front wheels suspended from a "gooseneck" frame allowed shorter turning than on previous tractors. It was built from 1914 through 1917, with more than 14,000 units made. That number exceeded all combined IH models previously made, making a strong argument for smaller tractors.

A slightly larger and more powerful 10/20 Mogul replaced the 8/16 in 1916, so both were available during parts of 1916 and 1917. The 10/20's larger 8½x12-inch (212.5x300-mm) single-cylinder engine was coupled to a two-speed gearbox. Fenders were another feature. Only about 9,000 of the 10/20 Moguls were made, perhaps due to the popularity of IH's other 10/20, the two-cylinder Titan, which was available through Deering dealers.

The Titan 10/20 was introduced in 1915. It had a twin-cylinder side-by-side 6½x8-inch (162.5x200-mm) horizontal engine running at up to 500 rpm, automobile-type steering of the two narrow-mounted front wheels, and two forward speeds of 2¼ mph and 2 7/8 mph (3.4 km/h and 4.6 km/h) with a reverse of 2 7/8 mph (4.6 km/h). The Titan 10/20 was a relatively lightweight tractor for its day at about 5,700 lb (2,565 kg). Thermosiphon circulation transferred engine heat to a top-mounted cooling tank. The Titans were painted gray with red wheels. More than 78,000 of the 10/20s were made between 1915 and 1922, making them the new IH tractor sales leader.

Unlike the "pop-pop-pause, pop-pop-pause" rhythm of the Deere two-cylinder machines, the Titan 10/20s had a regular exhaust note, due to their single-throw crank and regular power strokes every 360 degrees of crank rotation. With both of its pistons and rods changing directions simultaneously on every stroke, the Titan 10/20 created its own characteristic set of vibrations at some throttle settings.

The 10/20 might have sold even better but for the competition brought on by the Fordson, marketed from 1918 on. In the tractor price wars of the 1920s, Ford cut prices in 1922 to $395 for its two-plow Fordson. IH re-

1919 International Harvester 8/16

Four inline cylinders with overhead valves powered the new 8/16 IH kerosene tractor of 1917, the first American farm tractor with optional PTO. Based on a truck motor design, the tractor had its radiator and fan above the flywheel at the rear of the engine. This 1919 model, serial #VB5345, owned and restored by Merrill Sheets of Delaware, Ohio, was built late in 1919. IH offered an optional rear PTO on the 8/16, the first rear PTO in the United States.

What? What's that? How much? Two hundred and thirty dollars? Well, I'll be. . . . What'll we do about it? Do? Why damn it all, meet him, of course! We're going to stay in the tractor business. Yes, cut $230. Both models. Yes, both. And, say, listen, make it good! We'll throw in a plow as well.

—Alexander Legge, IH general manager responding to Ford's price wars, from Cyrus McCormick III, *The Century of the Reaper,* 1922

1910s International Harvester Motor Cultivator

Both photos: *Light motor cultivators were the rage in the 1915–1920 period. IH built fewer than 500 of its design between 1917 and 1920, before giving up on the concept. The IH model's rear motor mounted high above the single drive wheel made it top heavy, despite the wide, two-row-straddling front wheels. Wes Stratman of Pueblo, Colorado, collected this cultivator.*

The McCormick-Deering Farmalls have a record for performance and durability unequaled by any other tractors. They are the original row-crop tractors.
—Farmall ad, 1920s

1928 Farmall Regular

Above: *Kerosene fueled the two-plow Farmall through the field. A two-row cultivator mounted to the front brackets and was connected to the tractor steering through the short lever that projected from the front steering pedestal. That extra control helped the driver keep the cultivator centered over the rows. Cables connected to the front steering actuated wheel brakes to help shorten the turn of the Farmall into the next pair of rows at the field end.*

1928 Farmall Regular

Left: *The Farmall's distinctive rear-axle design provided the needed crop clearance. The wide drawbar came off before the cultivator was attached.*

The Row-Crop Tractor that does
All Farm Jobs *within Its Power Range.*
—Deere GPWT ad playing on the
Farmall name, 1930

1928 McCormick-Deering 10/20
Introduced in 1923, the McCormick-Deering 10/20 was a smaller version of the three-plow 15/30 brought out in 1921. Both tractors had single-piece cast frames and were powered with new engines that featured ball-bearing mains. Final drives were enclosed gear drives. Clem Seivert of Granger, Iowa, restored this 1928 10/20 from rusting remnants.

McCormick-Deering FARMALL All-Purpose Row-Crop Tractors

Illust. 52—Farmall 12.

Illust. 53—The Farmall-20 2-plow tractor.

Illust. 54—Farmall 30, the 3-plow size of the famous Farmall.

The McCormick-Deering Farmalls have a record for performance and durability unequaled by any other tractors. They are built in three sizes, and regardless of the size of the farm there is a Farmall or a combination of Farmalls to fit the requirements and supply most economical power. They are all-purpose tractors adapted to drawbar and belt work, and to planting and cultivating row crops. They are the original row-crop tractors.

The FARMALL 12 is the tractor for farms of up to 100 or more acres. It is also adapted to truck, dairy, and poultry farms. It has the power to plow deep—to make seedbeds as good as can be made with larger tractors. Quick-attachable machines available for direct attachment to the tractor include plows, middle-busters, two-row planters and cultivators, 7-foot mowers, 12-foot sweep rakes, etc.

The FARMALL 20 is the tractor for the average farm; that is, the farm of 160 or more acres where six to ten horses would be required to do the work. The original Farmall was introduced in 1924 and many of the tractors sold in 1924 and 1925 are still in use and going strong. The Farmall 20 is a direct descendant of that tractor, with 25 per cent more power and with other improvements which entitle it to the leadership it holds among tractors of this class —more than 200,000 of this size alone are in use.

The FARMALL 30 meets the requirements of farms in the 200- to 300-acre c'ass or where unusual soil conditions or heavier than usual loads call for a larger tractor. It supplies ample power to pull three or more plows, four-row cultivators, two-row corn pickers and potato diggers, harvester-threshers, etc.

Farmall tractors are regularly equipped with steel wheels but they can be equipped with pneumatic tires when wanted.

Operating a two-row middle buster.   Cultivating two rows.   Well adapted for farm work.

1930s Farmall lineup

sponded by reducing the price of the Titan 10/20 to $700, and added a three-bottom P & O plow to sweeten the deal; IH had recently purchased the Parlin & Orendorf Plow Company of Canton, Illinois.

Going Modern

The new 1917 IH 8/16 was almost streamlined in appearance. The engine housing tapered toward the front—where there was no radiator grill. The 8/16 was powered by a vertical four-cylinder 4x5-inch (100x125-mm) engine mounted lengthwise on the frame. Basically an engine similar to the IH Model G truck, the 8/16 revolved at up to 1,000 rpm. Engine cooling, as on the truck, was from a fan-blown radiator placed behind the engine. The engine had removeable cylinder sleeves and high-tension magneto ignition with impulse starter. The engine was coupled to the three-speed transmission with a multiple-disc dry clutch. Final drive was with roller chains to sprockets inside the rear wheels. Weight of the tractor was trimmed to about 3,300 lb (1,485 kg). It was rated as a two-plow tractor.

The 8/16 was produced as the VB, HC, and IC Series from 1917 through 1922. The IC Series had a 4½x5½-inch (112.5x137.5-mm) engine. According to available serial numbers, more than 33,000 of the model were produced with the later, more-powerful, version selling more than 16,500 units. The IC, too, had its price cut to $670, with a free two-bottom plow, to compete with the Fordson during the fierce price competition.

Modern was further defined with the 1921 introduction of the all-new McCormick-Deering 15/30 Gear Drive Tractor. Replacing the aged Titan 15/30 of 1914 vintage, the new tractor was of one-piece cast-iron frame construction; it added PTO capabilities, featured a new International four-cylinder engine with ball-bearing main bearings, and removeable cylinder sleeves. The 15/30's vertical four-cylinder engine, positioned lengthwise, had a bore and stroke of 4½x6 inches (112.5x150 mm), and operated at up to 1,000 rpm. The new 15/30 had a fully enclosed drivetrain with gear-driven rear wheels. The roller-chain final drive of previous models had been replaced. Wheel placement was configured in what is now called standard configuration. When it was upgraded in 1929, the 15/30's earlier version had already sold nearly 100,000 units.

The 1929 15/30 (later known as the 22/36) was a much-improved machine. IH increased the bore of the engine to 4¾ inches (119 mm) and its operating speed was boosted to 1,050 rpm. The 22/36 sold another 57,500 tractors from 1929 until its phase-out in 1934.

IH introduced its 8/16 replacement in 1923. The new 10/20 was a smaller version of the 15/30 with similar features, including the one-piece cast-iron frame and built-in PTO for powering drawn implements. The 10/20 was powered with another ball-bearing-main four-cylinder IH engine of 4¼x5 inches (106x125 mm) bore and stroke. Nebraska tests in 1927 showed 10.9 drawbar and 20.46 belt hp. Narrow-tread and orchard versions were made starting in 1925; rubber tires became an option in the mid-1930s. The two-plow 10/20 became one of the most popular tractors of its time, with more than 215,000 sold between 1923 and 1939; its production peaked in 1929 at nearly 40,000 machines.

The Revolutionary Farmall

Most tractor companies, including IH, had developed and built lightweight motor cultivators starting about 1915. International's Motor Cultivator of 1916 was a 15-hp backward-running tricycle with the four-cylinder motor mounted crosswise above the single rear driving wheel. The rear drive wheel and the engine assembly pivoted at the frame for steering. Cultivator shovels were mounted just behind the two front wheels, and the operator sat just above the cultivator and in front of the engine. Farmer acceptance of the motor cultivator concept was poor across the board. Farmers clung to their horse cultivators for such critical tasks as cultivating row crops, and they resisted buying another machine that could only cultivate.

IH engineers realized there was potential for a machine that could do *all* of the power work on the farm, a real general-purpose tractor. Leftover Motor Cultivators—and IH had some—became test vehicles as carriers for all sorts of mounted equipment. Engineering work finally evolved into a front-running tricycle onto which a two-row cultivator could be mounted and then steered effectively from the rear operator's seat.

IH started calling it the Farmall before it was officially named or the trademark registered. Twenty-two prototypes were put together in 1923 and sent to the field for testing. After years of constant tests, tweaks, and more tests, 205 Farmalls were hand-assembled in 1924 and put on the market. They were well accepted.

Production of the Farmall began in earnest in 1925, with more than 800 made. The figure for 1926 rose to 4,418; in 1927 to 9,501; in 1928 to 24,898; in 1929 to 35,320; and production peaked at 42,092 Farmalls in 1930. Total production for the Farmall "Regular" was close to 126,000 from 1924 through 1932. The peak production years coincided with Ford's throwing in the towel and moving Fordson production out of the United States to Ireland. IH regained its lead in tractor sales on the strength of a new machine that firmly established row-crop tractors as the dominant farm tractor type.

The two-plow Farmall of 1924 was available with a front-mounted two-row cultivator, a rear-mounted mower, mounted middle breaker, and other attachments true to the farm-all concept. The engine was an IH four-cylinder of 3¾x5 inches (94x125 mm) bore and stroke running at up to 1,200 rpm. International didn't rate the tractor initially, fearing competition with its own machines, specifically its 10/20. When tested at Nebraska in 1925, the Farmall showed 9.35 drawbar and 18.3 belt hp.

Unique to the Farmall at its introduction was its high-standing, crop-clearing, tricycle configuration. Its patented cultivator guidance was steering-connected to shift cultivator gangs quickly, and cable-actuated steering brakes facilitated short turns into the next row-pair at the end of the field. Belt pulley and PTO added to the overall utility of the Farmall. IH was really onto something—a practical general-purpose tractor. Other manufacturers hustled to make their own row-crops.

A big brother of the Farmall, the F-30 Farmall debuted in late 1931. Power was upgraded to three-plow size with a four-cylinder 4¼x5-inch (106x125-mm) engine operating at up to 1,150 rpm. The F-30 weighed close to 5,300 lb (2,385 kg) and could turn around in an 18-foot (540-cm) circle. By 1936, the F-30 was available on factory-installed pneumatic rubber tires with a new high-speed gear for road transit. The F-30 was built from 1931 through 1939, with nearly 29,000 tractors made. W-30 standard-tread versions of the tractor sold another 32,000 units. Industrial I-30s and the W-30s were made from 1932 to 1939. Beginning in 1936, IH tractors were painted the now-familiar Farmall Red.

The original Farmall Regular was replaced with the F-20 in 1932. Much like the Regular, the F-20 was slightly larger with power that had been boosted about 10 percent; Nebraska tests show 16.12 belt and 24.13 drawbar hp. The F-20's four-speed transmission gave it operating speeds of 2¼ mph, 2¾ mph, 3¼ mph, and 3¾ mph (3.6 km/h, 4.4 km/h, 5.2 km/h, and 6 km/h). In the mid-1930s, the F-20 was made available on rubber tires. Sometime during 1936, its gray paint was changed to red. Options for the later F-20s included adjustable wide fronts, wheel weights, mechanical or hydraulic lifts, and electric starter and lights. The F-20 was produced in record numbers (nearly 149,000) when production ended in 1939.

A Baby Farmall

The small F-12 Farmall was introduced in 1932. Rated as a one-to-two-plow tractor, the F-12 took the row-crop tractor design to its final form. Long rear axles with a machined-in keyway permitted the rear wheels to be adjusted to any width by first loosening the hub bolts, then sliding the wheels on the axles to the desired setting. The F-12's four-cylinder 3x4-inch (75x100-mm) engine had an operating speed of 1,400 rpm. Nebraska tests showed 12.31 drawbar and 16.2 belt hp for the gas-burning tractor.

Equipment made for the F-12 included two-row mounted cultivators, rear-mounted PTO-driven mowers, and mounted planters, plows and other implements. Quick-Attach features speeded changeover between implements or back to the drawbar: long toggle bolts flipped over the tractor axlehousing, dropped into slots on the clamps, and secured the attachment. A single-

1936 Farmall F-30

Above: *A bigger Farmall rolled down the rows in 1931. The F-30, a three-plow scale-up of the original Farmall (now called the Regular), could handle four-row equipment. Harold Glaus of Nashville, Tennessee, restored this 1936 Model F-30 that his father bought and used in 1942, just before Harold was born. The tires, on French & Hecht wheels, went on in 1943 and they're still rolling. The F-30 was made from 1931 to 1939.*

1935 Farmall F-12

Left: *Fenders and a mechanical lift added to the ease and safety of driving this 1935 Farmall F-12. The little Farmall came out in 1932 and filled the niche for a smaller, lower-priced tractor. Rubber tires cost extra in 1935, so many tractors were still delivered on steel wheels. Kerosene versions of the F-12 had a small tank in the hood to hold starting gas. Retired dairyman Rex Miller of Savannah, Missouri, fixed up this 1935 model.*

1939 Farmall F-14
The F-12 was replaced in 1938 by the slightly larger 14/17-hp F-14, which was made only until 1939. This 1939 F-14 was fixed up by John Bossler, of Highland, Illinois. Bossler's is fitted with adjustable wide front.

purpose wrench with an offset crank handle speeded up the job of tightening the clamps.

Rubber tires were made available as a factory-installed option early on, as was a special road gear for rubber-tired F-12s. The regular three-speed transmission provided ground speeds of 2¼ mph, 3 mph, and 3¾ mph (3.6 km/h, 4.8 km/h, and 6 km/h).

The F-12 was another IH success. A total of 123,407 F-12s were made from 1932 to 1938. A standard version, the W-12, was available from 1934 to 1938, but only 3,617 W-12s were made. The O-12 orchard tractor was available from 1935 to 1938, and sold nearly 2,400 units. Another version, the Fairway-12, was built for golf courses and other turf operations.

The F-12 was replaced in 1938 with the F-14. The F-14 was much like the earlier F-12, but IH speeded up the engine to 1,650 rpm compared with 1,400 rpm on the F-12. The F-14 on rubber tires tested out at 14.84 drawbar and 17.44 belt hp at Nebraska. Standard, Fairway, and orchard versions of the Model 14 were available during 1938 and 1939. Total F-14 production was 27,396, with another 1,900 tractors made in the standard-tread versions.

Make Way for Diesels and Crawlers
Big farmers now had big tractors: IH added to its big standard tractor line in 1934 with the six-cylinder W-40 and WD-40. The W-40 gas engine was the first six-cylinder-engined IH tractor. The 3¾x4½-inch (94x112.5-mm) engine could burn kerosene or distil-

1939 Farmall F-20

Above: *A Farmall slightly larger than the Regular arrived in 1932. Designated the F-20, it replaced the original Farmall. This sparkling 1939 Farmall F-20 was built in 1939, the last year of production. Unlike the regular, the F-20's worm-and-sector gearing on the steering column is enclosed. The cleaner was still front-mounted. Owner-restorer Tom Hill of Piqua, Ohio, has equipped this tractor with nearly all the options available in 1939. Front to back are an adjustable wide front, radiator shutter, direct-drive generator with starter and lights, wheel weights, and fenders. Tom Hill hunted for parts for seven years in eight states before he found all he needed to complete his F-20.*

1939 Farmall F-20 controls

Left: *F-20 production ended in 1939, after a production run of nearly 140,000 tractors. The F-20 produced 16/24 hp at its Nebraska test, about 10 percent more than the Regular.*

late. Nebraska tests rated it 35.22 drawbar and 49.76 belt hp.

The WD-40 diesel was the first U.S. diesel-powered wheel-type tractor. The WD-40 did about as well as the gas W-40, with 37.21 drawbar and 48.79 belt hp. Both were available on rubber or steel. The W-40 was the more-popular unit and 6,454 units were made, while only 3,370 of the diesels came out between 1934 and 1940. Industrial versions of the gas and diesel 40s were made from 1936 to 1940.

Crawler tractors entered the IH line in 1928 with a small machine based on the 10/20 tractor. The 10/20 TracTracTor was built in only 1,504 units until it was updated as the T-20 in 1931. The T/20 TracTracTor weighed in at 6,725 lb (3,025 kg) and ran the 10/20 engine at a faster clip of 1,250 rpm. It was built between 1931 and 1939, and was the most popular of the IH farm-sized crawlers, with 15,198 units produced.

Larger crawlers, the TA-40 and diesel TD-40, were produced from 1932 to 1934 in numbers totaling 1,312 tractors. They were then replaced with the T-40 and TD-40 built between 1934 and 1939. The 40 Series crawlers used the same engines as the W-40s. Nebraska tests showed the 40s pulling more than 40 drawbar hp. More than 7,060 of these tractors were made.

More than 5,580 Model T-35 and TD-35 TracTracTors were also produced from 1937 through 1939. The T-35 was an in-between-sized tractor that could pull 35 drawbar hp. The small farm crawlers built before 1940 formed the base for IH's later entry into the industrial crawler market.

A Brand New Look

Sharp corners and square fronts were smoothed and rounded starting in the late 1930s. Famed industrial designer Raymond Loewy began with a facelift of the IH company trademark and moved on to improve the

1939 McCormick-Deering W-40

A big, new six-cylinder engine was used by IH for the first time in a tractor in its W-40 standard tread introduced in 1934. Another version, the WD-40 also debuted in 1934 and was the first wheel-type tractor in this country powered by a diesel engine. The WD-40's four-cylinder IH engine could be crank-started on gasoline and then switched over to diesel. This 1939 W-40 was rejuvenated by its owner, Powell Smith of Shelbyville, Tennessee.

1940 Farmall H

Above: *The all-new Farmall Models H, M, A, and B debuted in 1939, with slick styling from industrial designer Raymond Loewy. This H is the two-plow tractor that replaced the F-20 in the IH product line. Rear-wheel tread adjustment on the new series was by a sliding hub, similar to that used on the earlier F-12 and F-14 models. Roland Henik of Mt. Vernon, Iowa, restored this 1940 H that his father bought new.*

Right: **1940s Farmall advertisement**

tractors' looks and operation. The big new 80-hp TD-18 crawler introduced in 1938 was the first unit that showed the Loewy touch. The distinctive rounded radiator grill with its horizontal slits soon dressed up all of the crawler line, including the smaller T-6, TD-6, T-9, TD-9, T-14, and TD-14.

The big news from IH in 1939 was its spanking-new line of Farmall tractors wearing the Loewy styling. The largest, the Farmall M, was to achieve later fame as one of the classic American tractors.

The new, small-engined Farmalls were the A and B, which shared the same engine but had different appeal. The A was a small machine with wide-set adjustable-tread front wheels. Its engine and drivetrain were offset to the left of the frame. The operator sat at the right of the engine for a better view of the cultivator; this new design was called Culti-Vision. The B was similarly configured with Culti-Vision, but it was supplied with a tricyle front and more tread adjustability for cultivating two rows.

The 3x4-inch (75x100-mm) engines in the A and B showed 13 drawbar and 16 belt hp on gas; the distillate tests were nearly 2 hp less. Engines in both models ran at up to 1,400 rpm. Combined, the A and B accounted for more than 218,000 unit sales during production from 1939 through 1947.

The new M and H shared the same wheelbase for implement interchangeability, but the H had a smaller engine. The three-plow M had optional electric starting and lights, belt pulley and PTO, and hydraulic Lift-All. Rubber tires were standard, but the tractor could be ordered on steel wheels for less money. The gas M produced 25.83 drawbar and 33.35 belt hp in its Nebraska tests; the M kerosene results were somewhat lower. The M engine was of 3⅞x5¼ inches (97x131 mm) bore and stroke and was designed to operate at 1450 rpm. The MD diesel first appeared in 1941. Like the earlier IH diesel engines, the MD started on gas and switched to diesel once it was running. More than 297,000 Ms and its specialized versions were manufactured from 1939 to 1952. The McCormick-Deering standard version in the M size was the W-6 and WD-6. It was also made as the OS-6 and O-6 in orchard modifications.

The two-plow H had the same equipment options as the larger M. Its 3⅝x4¼-inch (91x106-mm) engine ran at up to 1,650 rpm. In Nebraka tests, the gas version of the H showed 19.13 drawbar and 23.72 belt hp; the kerosene version showed a couple of horsepower less in each category. In total production between 1939 and 1952, the H came out in more than 391,000 units, surpassing the M by nearly 100,000 tractors.

Farmall H counterparts in standard tractors were the McCormick-Deering W-4, OS-4, and O-4 models. The OS-4 had the exhaust and air cleaner undermounted to reduce its height for orchard work. The O-4 had complete shielding of the rear tires and operator platform to protect orchard and grove trees. Both models were available with many of the Farmall's options.

IH's big farm tractor of the 1940s was the McCormick-Deering W-9 standard of four-plow size with a muscular 50 drawbar hp. It was available as a diesel, WD-9, and in rice field versions WR-9 and WRD-9. The W-9 was marketed between 1940 and 1953, and more than 67,000 were made.

World War II shifted farm equipment production into defense item production. Steel wheels temporarily replaced rubber tires until synthetics were available. New model introductions were rare, and tractor production nearly ceased. Postwar, materials were scarce, so it took time for the farm equipment industry to supply the pent-up demand.

Cubs and Cs

Two different-sized Farmalls replaced the B in 1947. They were the Farmall Cub and the Farmall C. The Cub was a tiny Farmall meant for one-row cultivation and estate manicures. It could pull about 9 drawbar hp with its 2⅝x2¾-inch (66x69-mm) engine turning at up to 1,600 rpm. The Cub featured the offset engine and drivetrain for improved Culti-Vision. More than 185,000 were made from 1947 to 1954.

The C was a modernized tricyle row-crop with improved Touch-Control hydraulics to ease the operation of its attached implements. Unlike its predecessor, the C's engine, drivetrain, and operator seat were all centered in line. Visibility to the two-row attachments was enhanced by narrowed frame components ahead and below the operator's line of sight. The handy little C was built in numbers approaching 80,000 during its manufacture from 1948 to 1951.

More Power for the Fifties

Farmers were clamoring for increased horsepower to power their larger farms more efficiently as the 1950s dawned. Outside suppliers offered power kits to soup-up engines until tractor makers joined the power race.

The Super M with Torque Amplifier or Super MTA was built from 1952 to 1954. The TA was also added to

the Super MD and the Super W-6. The TA provided two speeds in each transmission gear, giving the Super M and the other TA-equipped tractors the equivalent of ten forward and two reverse speeds. Lever-operated, the TA could be engaged on the go to reduce speed about one-third but increase pulling power by 48 percent. The operator could also shift back up to the previous speed without stopping. IH also offered live PTO on its new tractors. PTO-driven implements could now be run independently of tractor ground travel. Hydraulic implement control was also increasingly available, first as remote cylinders, then coupled with lift arms on the tractor.

First of the Super Series was the Super C produced from 1951 to 1954. Its four-cylinder 3⅛x4-inch (78x100-mm) engine furnished 20.72 drawbar and 23.67 belt hp when tested at Nebraska, a couple horsepower higher than the older C. In 1953, a two-point Fast-Hitch, designed to compete with the three-point Ford-Ferguson hitch, was made available on the Super C. The Super C also offered optional adjustable wide-front tread. More than 98,000 Super Cs were made before the tractor became the Farmall 200 in 1954.

The A became the Super A in 1952, while the B was dropped in 1947. The H became the Super H in 1953, with an improvement in power output to 30.69 drawbar and 33.4 belt hp. The H was replaced in 1954 by the Farmall three-plow 300 that offered Fast-Hitch and Torque Amplifier.

The Super M's successor was the Farmall 400 built from 1954 to 1956. It was available with Fast-Hitch and Hydro-Touch hydraulics in either gas or diesel. The W-400 and WD-400 were the 400's standard-tread versions. The 400's 4x5½-inch (100x137.5-mm) engine showed 45.34 drawbar and 50.78 belt hp on gas in Nebraska tests.

International 300 utility tractors became available

1940 Farmall M with No-Till Planter
The Purdue University Ag Engineering department restored this classic 1940 Farmall M and 1953 IH M-21 Till-Planter to mark the school's contributions to No-Till farming methods. Initial work on the planter began at Purdue in West Lafayette, Indiana, and was continued by IH.

1941 McCormick Deering O-4

Above: *This 1941 McCormick-Deering O-4 had orchard shielding that let the H-sized tractor slip through orchards without damaging blooms, trees, or fruit. Brothers Phil, Bill, and Glen Steward of Springport, Michigan, spent months restoring and hammering out the sheetmetal before they added the O-4 to their tractor collection.*

1941 Farmall MD

Facing page, top: *The fuel economy of diesel-engined row-crop tractors was available for the first time with the 1941 Farmall MD. The panel in the front grill could be removed to install a cultivator shift lever for shifting gang cultivators. Alan Smith of McHenry, Illinois, knew this tractor from his youth, when a neighbor owned it. Smith later bought it and fixed it up.*

1941 Farmall MD

Facing page, bottom: *Starting the MD was relatively easy. The engine started on gasoline and was shifted over to diesel with the levers just left of the steering wheel. This MD originally cost about $1,550 compared with $1,112 for the gas M. Cast wheel weights were popular options.*

starting in 1955. Their low profile and standard tread made them an ideal loader tractor. The utility series became popular on livestock farms where they were the chore tractor and could be pressed into tillage and planting work when the season demanded.

The Super A became the 100 in 1955. The 100 Series tractors had a restyled grill with central vertical slots added to the widened horizontal slots. Model numbering and the Farmall or International name was in chromed letters and numerals. The IH logo, also in chrome, was prominently displayed on the top front of the radiator grill.

In 1956, the Farmall 130, 230, 350, and 450 replaced their even-numbered models of the previous year. A cream color was used in the paint scheme as a backing for the Farmall trademark on the hoods and as a contrast on the radiator grill. The 130 replaced the 100, the 230 the 200, the 350 the 300, and the 450 the 400. Power was increased on all of the tractors. The International 330 utility, replacing the 300, came along in 1957.

Major product improvements were part of the 1958 model lineup. The Farmall 140, 240, 340, 460, and 560 featured all-new styling. The radiator grill was squared off with bold horizontal bars. The cream accent now swept back from the grill and shroud to the sides of the hood. The 460 and 560 came with six-cylinder engines in gas or diesel, the first IH six-cylinder row-crop tractors. The hydraulic pump, by now a serious part of tractor systems, was moved inside the transmission case from the previous engine-block location. A crankcase oil cooler was added to help dispel heat from the hardworking engines. Steering was reconfigured from the over-the-top position of the early Farmall; the shaft was now placed along the engine siderail. There it connected to a worm drive inside the front bolster where steering was hydraulically aided. Neat instrument consoles were positioned near the steering wheel. Seat backrests addressed operator comfort

In 1960, IH continued with many improvements to the Farmall line. The new 404 and 504 boasted the first American-designed three-point hitch with draft sensing. In 1959, industry standards for three-point hitches were adopted to enhance implement interchangeabilty between makes. IH took its crankcase cooler another step forward and used it also to cool hydraulic fluid. A dry air cleaner for better operation and easier servicing was adopted. And IH adopted hydrostatic power steering to the 504.

Although it didn't completely replace the tricycle-type tractor, adjustable wide-front tread was available on more row-crop Farmalls. With industry adoption of the three-point hitch in 1959, more implements were mounted on the tractor's rear as integral hitches. That included rear-mounted cultivators, so there was no longer the pressing need to mount cultivators in front of the tractor beside the quick-turning tricycle front.

Rapid Changes Toward the Future

Bold new advances in engineering, power, design, and manufacturing marked the next two decades for IH. Diesel engines gained popularity and were increasingly tweaked to produce more power and better efficiency. Turbocharging crammed more oxygen into the new engines; intercooling was added to make the turbocharged air more dense. Transmissions became more sophisticated with the need to transmit more power. First mechanical, or hydraulic front wheel assist, then four-wheel drive was used increasingly as available horsepower passed 150 and headed toward 200. Factory-built cabs were added to the larger machines.

Innovation continued and in 1979, International's 2+2 articulated four-wheel-drive row-crop tractor was introduced, available as the 130-hp 3388 or the 150-hp 3588. The 2+2's unique design positioned the engine in front of the front axle on the forward segment of the "hinged" design. The operator sat in a cab over the rear wheels. The 2+2 promised a nimble row-crop machine with a highly productive large-horsepower size.

Fate of the Famous Farmalls

Events conspired against the future of International Harvester. The 1980s farm crisis disrupted the farm economy. Kicked off by a grain export embargo, interest rates peaked above 20 percent, land prices plunged, and farmers quit buying equipment. And then IH experienced a six-month strike. Company losses reached $397 million for fiscal 1980. By 1981, IH's 150th anniversary year, IH losses were at $393 million. In 1982, losses mounted to a disastrous $1.638 billion. Losses in 1983 were reduced to $485 million, but despite its efforts, IH couldn't turn itself around.

In late 1984, Tenneco Inc. bought the agricultural equipment division of IH and brought it into its J. I. Case subsidiary. The merged name was changed to Case-International the next year. International Harvester and its famous Farmalls were no more.

1941 McCormick-Deering O-4
Above: *The Steward brothers preserve their old farm buildings as well as their classic tractors.*

1941 McCormick Deering O-4 controls
Left: *The O-4 operator's seat and platform provided protection from low branches. The O-4 was introduced with the other styled IH tractors in 1939.*

1941 Farmall A
Above: *Culti-Vision was featured on the Farmall A in 1939. Torque-tube frame construction as well as the offset engine and drivetrain gave the operator full view of the undermounted cultivator. Alton and Thalua Garner of Levelland, Texas, restored this 1941 Farmall A from a rusting collection of parts they bought in New Mexico.*

1941 Farmall A controls
Right: *Designed for smaller farms and truck gardening, the Farmall A gave the operator a convenient grouping of controls.*

1949 Farmall Cub

Above: *Smallest of the Farmalls was the Cub. It was built continuously with only minor changes from 1947 to 1979, setting a record thirty-two-year production life for one model. Lawrance N. Shaw, professor of Agricultural Engineering at the University of Florida at Gainesville, uses his 1949 Cub to pull an automatic vegetable transplanter he's developing.*

1959 Farmall 560 Diesel

Left: *This 560 Farmall diesel shows thirty-four years of evolution since the tractor's beginning in 1924. The 560 D was a popular, powerful machine with the first IH six-cylinder diesel in a row-crop tractor. Farmall 560s were five-plow tractors that produced about 60 drawbar hp. This 1959 560 D was remade to like-new condition by farm-equipment-maker Jon Kinzenbaw of Williamsburg, Iowa.*

Sure Footed Power.
—IH TracTracTor ad, 1950s

Chapter 8

Massey-Ferguson

*A team that does more work at lower cost!
Massey-Harris tractors and mounted equip-
ment save time, save labor, save soil.*
—Massey-Harris ad, 1949

Above: **1938 Massey-Harris 101**

1938 Massey-Harris 101
Left: *The all-new Massey-Harris 101 arrived in 1938.
Streamlined from front to back, the tractor's engine was also
new behind the louvered side panels. The 101's powerplant
was a high-compression gas-burning Chrysler L-head six-
cylinder. Richard Prince of Conover, Ohio, rescued his
"sleeping beauty" from a collapsed barn, and restored it to a
new life.*

Massey-Ferguson is the shortened name of Massey-Harris-Ferguson, Ltd., formed in 1953 when Massey-Harris Company merged with Harry Ferguson, Inc. Ferguson was the inventive Irishman, who together with Henry Ford, created the 1939 Ford-Ferguson 9N tractor with its hydraulic draft-sensing three-point implement hitch.

The 1891 merger of the Massey Manufacturing Company of Toronto and the A. Harris, Son & Company Ltd. of Brantford, Ontario, put together the Massey-Harris Company, Canada's largest agricultural equipment firm. The Massey firm has roots tracing back to Daniel Massey and his start in 1847 making simple farm implements. Alanson Harris started about ten years later making similar tools. The two companies had each grown to the point where they were number one and two in Canadian farm equipment sales. As Massey-Harris, the company continued to add Canadian firms, and in 1910, got into the U.S. market with the purchase of Johnston Harvester Company of Batavia, New York.

Massey Gets Serious About Tractors

Massey-Harris sold about every other farm implement, but it needed a tractor to become a full-line company. It had sold the Bull tractor for a short time starting in 1917, but the Bull's plummeting popularity doomed that effort. The next tractor Massey handled was that of the Parrett Tractor Company of Chicago. Massey's Parrett Models No. 1, No. 2, and No. 3 were assembled by M-H in Weston, Ontario, between 1918 and 1923. The ubiquitous Fordson was making inroads into all companies' tractor sales, and when it was imported into Canada, the Fordson effectively killed the Parrett there, as it had in the United States.

In 1926, Massey began to negotiate marketing rights for the Wallis tractor with J. I. Case Plow Works of Racine, Wisconsin. The Plow Works was separate from the J. I. Case Threshing Machine Company of the same city. Beginning as early as 1902, plow works president Henry M. Wallis, J. I. Case's son-in-law, was working on a big tractor made in Cleveland, Ohio, called the Wallis Bear. The Wallis Tractor Company was merged into the Case Plow Works in 1919, and the Wallis tractor was developed into an early practical tractor that was relatively lightweight and powered by a four-cylinder engine mounted lengthwise on the frame.

The Wallis Tractor Heritage

From its start about 1902, the Wallis Bear was a massive machine built as a 20/50 and a 40/80 giant designed to do only the big jobs. But compared with the other gas tractors of its day, it was relatively modern. The Bear started as a four-cylinder design with the radiator-cooled engine mounted lengthwise. The Bear's 1912 version had slimmed down to 10½ tons (9,450 kg) and was rated at 30 drawbar and 50 belt hp. Its 7½x9-inch (187.5x225-mm) engine chugged along at up to 650 rpm. Only nine of that model are known to have been built.

Wallis cut the tractor size and horsepower in half for its next model, the 1912 Wallis Cub. It, too, had a four-cylinder vertical engine positioned lengthwise. The Cub featured an early use of unit-frame construction: a boilerplate crankcase and transmission housing that served as its frame. It was rated as a 26/44 from its 650-rpm engine that could burn gas, kerosene, or distillate. Like its Bear predecessors, the Cub featured one wheel in front, with the belt pulley in the rear.

In 1915, the Cub's size was reduced by half again in the Cub Jr. or Model J. It was a 13/25 tractor with a 4½x5¾-inch (112.5x137.5-mm) engine, and was improved in design with the boilerplate unit frame housing the engine crankcase, transmission, and differential. All drive components were fully enclosed—quite a feat for a 1915 machine. The belt pulley was squeezed into a position on the tractor's left side between the wheel and transmission housing.

Wallis based subsequent tractors on the successful Cub Jr., but dropped the single front wheel in favor of two wheels with automotive-type steering on its Model K of 1919. The 1922 Wallis OK was tested at Nebraska in 1922 and turned out 18 drawbar and 28 belt hp from its 4¼x5¾-inch (106x144-mm) engine at 1,000 rpm. By 1922, the tractor weighed 4,000 lb (1,800 kg). More engine speed and other tweaking turned the 1927 Wallis OK into a 20/30 tractor. Massey first sold it as the Wallis 20/30 "certified," under a marketing agreement with Wallis.

Massey Buys a Tractor Line

After first selling the Wallis tractors in Canada and parts of the United States under an agreement with the Case Plow Works, Massey-Harris bought the entire company in 1928 and acquired not only the Wallis tractor line, but the company's plows and other implements as well. One thing Massey-Harris didn't need out of the deal was the Case name. Massey subsequently sold to Case Threshing Machine all rights to the Case and J. I. Case monikers.

In 1929, Massey brought out an upgraded Wallis 20/30 as its Wallis 26/41, or Model 25. It also introduced

1916 Sawyer-Massey

The Sawyer-Massey Company of Hamilton, Ontario, Canada, was a well-known maker of steam engines and threshing machines that dated back to the late 1800s. Gas tractors followed in 1910. Although not a part of corporate Massey-Harris, Sawyer-Massey was linked to the Massey family through the family's investments in the firm. This 1916 Sawyer-Massey 20/40 is owned by Thomas Stewart of Woodstock, Ontario.

1912 Wallis Bear

Above: *This huge 1912 Wallis Bear fathered a line of tractors that started Massey in the tractor business. The Bear was rated at 30/50 hp and could pull eight to ten plow bottoms. Collector Eugene Schmidt of Bluffton, Ohio, restored serial #203 in 1962. The tractor was originally sold in London, Ohio, the only one thought to have ended up east of the Mississippi River.*

1912 Wallis Bear power steering

Right: *Friction-drive power steering helped turn the front wheels on the 10½-ton (9,450-kg) Wallis Bear. Pushing in or pulling out on the steering wheel activated the power mechanism to help turn the front wheel left or right.*

1916 Wallis Cub Jr.
Above: *A boilerplate U-shaped unit frame held everything together on the small 1916 Wallis Cub Jr., developed from its big brother the Wallis Cub. The Cub Jr.'s drive components were all enclosed, and roller bearings were used extensively to help this reliable two-speed 15/27-hp machine. Dick Carroll of Alta Vista, Kansas, restored this Cub Jr.*

1918 Massey-Harris MH-1
Left: *Massey-Harris started selling its versions of the Chicago, Illinois, Parret tractor in 1918. Massey assembled the MH-1, MH-2, and MH-3 in its Weston, Ontario, Canada, plant. This 12/22-hp MH-1 is driven by Lawrence Myers of Dallas Center, Iowa.*

Most Acres for Your Dollar!
—Wallis Cub ad, 1918

1930 Wallis 12/20
Above: *The 12/20 Wallis of 1930 evolved into the standard-tread Massey Pacemaker of 1936. Massey owned Wallis from 1928 on, but sold tractors under the Wallis name. This 12/20 Wallis belongs to Richard and Carlene Meyer of Dudley, Massachusetts.*

1930 Massey-Harris General-Purpose
Right: *Designed as Massey's general-purpose row-crop tractor, the 1930 four-wheel-drive GP came in four tread widths to match different row spacings. The front wheels steered through universal joints and the rear wheels followed. The rear axle oscillated near the differential to handle uneven ground. Raymond Krukewitt of Sidney, Illinois, spent a winter restoring this GP.*

a smaller version, the 12/20. The 12/20 had a less-powerful engine with 3⅞x5¼ inches (97x131 mm) bore and stroke that drove a three-speed transmission. Weight was down to 3,432 lb (1,545 kg).

In 1930, M-H announced its all-new four-wheel-drive General Purpose tractor. Four tread widths were available for different row-crop spacings. Row-crop clearance was provided by way of gear drop boxes from the axles to the wheels. The front wheels turned to steer the tractor with power transmitted through universal joints. The rear-axle assembly pivoted at the rear differential housing to allow its four wheels to stay in contact with the ground on uneven terrain. A two-row cultivator was available. By 1936, an improved General Purpose was offered, now equipped with rubber tires.

The Massey Challenger, a two-to-three-plow tricycle row-crop tractor debuted in 1936. It was a 26/36 tractor with adjustable rear wheels for different row widths. It

still used the U-channel boilerplate unit frame of its Wallis ancestors, but was available on rubber or steel wheels. The Challenger featured a streamlined cast grill.

The Twin-Power Pacemaker of 1937 was another transitional tractor caught between Wallis and M-H designs. It had a high-compression engine designed to burn high, 68–70-octane gasoline. Its Twin-Power feature produced two power output ratings by governing the engine at either 1,200 or 1,400 rpm.

In 1938, the row-crop Challenger also had Twin-Power; it became the last of the Wallis-type tractors.

Massey Builds its Own Tractors

In 1938, Massey brought out the red M-H 101 row-crop with cast frame and sheetmetal streamlining. It was powered by a Chrysler-made six-cylinder L-head engine designed to thrive on high-test gas. The M-H 101 was also available in a standard, or wheatland, version. Both machines had the Twin-Power feature.

A wartime model, the M-H 81, was pressed into service on Royal Canadian Air Force bases as an aircraft tow tractor. The row-crop version was built from 1941 to 1948 and the standard version from 1941 to 1946. The M-H 81 was powered by a Continental four-cylinder 3x4⅜-inch (75x109-mm) engine. Only about 6,000 were made. It was followed in 1947 by the M-H 20, a one-to-two-plow tractor designed for the lighter work on the farm.

Another 1947 entry was the 30, a two-plow tractor available in row-crop or standard tread with a five-speed transmission. Its Continental L-head engine turned at up to 1,500 rpm for drawbar work or 1,800 rpm for belt applications. The 30 was upgraded to the 33 and 333 during its production from 1947 to 1953; more than 32,000 units were made during that time period.

The 30's larger stablemates for 1947 included the three-plow M-H 44 available with four- or six-cylinder gas engines or a four-cylinder diesel, and the M-H 55, a four-plow tractor for the big jobs. The 55 had a 60-hp engine and was available in gas or diesel. The 55 was made from 1947 to 1956, when about 21,000 were built. More than 95,000 Model 44s were sold during its production life from 1947 to 1955.

The small Pony tractor was introduced by M-H in 1947. Smallest in the line, the Pony could pull one small plow or do many other light duties on the farm or acreage. Its 2⅜x3½-inch (59x87.5-mm) Continental engine spun at up to 1,800 rpm to deliver about 10 drawbar and 11 PTO hp. It was built between 1947 and 1954 in Canada, with more than 27,000 tractors made.

1949 Massey-Harris 44 advertisement
Above: *In 1947, Massey launched the three-plow 44 and the four-plow 55.*

1938 Massey-Harris Challenger
Facing page, top: *Massey's first tricycle row-crop was the 1936 Challenger. The rounded cast grill was Massey's first attempt at streamlining. This 26/36 tractor marked the last of the Wallis-type tractors and their boilerplate unit frame. This 1938 Challenger was masterfully restored by collector Kurt Kelsey of Iowa Falls, Iowa.*

1942 Massey-Harris 81
Facing page, bottom: *Only about 6,000 Massey-Harris Model 81 tractors were made due to production limits imposed during World War II. Standard-tread versions were made between 1941 and 1946; row-crops from 1941 to 1948. None were made in 1943. Ronald Hoffmeister of Altamont, Illinois, found his 1942 row-crop model near home, and restored it to like-new condition.*

Ferguson Joins the Fold

The year 1953 marked the start of many changes at Massey, as the merger with Harry Ferguson created Massey-Harris-Ferguson. Some of the Massey-Harris tractors were updated and continued in production. Initially, the tractors were sold through either Massey-Harris or Ferguson dealerships as separate product lines. Later, dealerships were consolidated.

In 1953, the M-H 33 became the 33 RT gas. Its Nebraska tests showed 35.54 drawbar and 39.52 belt hp. It was also available as a diesel. The 33 RT was produced between 1953 and 1957. The M-H 44 Special was a gas standard tractor that delivered 43.58 drawbar and 48.95 belt hp. It, too, was available with a diesel engine. The M-H No. 16 Pacer of 1954–1957 was a larger version of the Pony, with 17 drawbar hp.

The M-H's upgraded 555 gas and diesel tractors replaced the Model 55 in 1955. The 555 offered Depth-O-Matic, the Massey-Ferguson equivalent of the Ferguson System of hydraulic lift and implement control. On the Ferguson-derived machines, the hydraulic system was called Hydramic Power.

Under the new merger, M-H continued to build Ferguson tractors as well. The Ferguson TO-35 of 1955 was made in Ferguson's Detroit plant. The TO-35's 2,000-rpm $3\frac{5}{16}$x$3\frac{7}{8}$-inch (83x97-mm) Continental engine rated 30 drawbar hp via a six-speed transmission. The TO-35 later graduated into the MF-35, painted red and gray.

The year 1956 brought the Ferguson gas 40 and the Massey gas 50. Identical under the skin, these tractors both had the same 134-ci (2195-cc) Continental engine, and put out just over 30 drawbar hp. LPG and diesel versions of the M-H 50 were offered, and the model was made from 1956 through 1965. In 1956, Massey also updated the 33 to the 333, and offered it for gas, diesel, or LPG. The M-H 444 of 1956 to 1958 became available with LPG- and diesel-engine options. Both the 333 and 444 offered Depth-O-Matic.

By 1958, Massey-Ferguson offered tractor models ranging from 25 to 60 hp with diesel or gas engines. Larger tractors followed.

Perkins Diesel Addition

Diesel engine maker F. Perkins Ltd., of Peterborough, Ontario, was bought by Massey-Ferguson in 1959. Perkins had been supplying diesels to Massey-Harris since 1947, when its engines first powered the M-H 44.

A three-cylinder Perkins diesel was offered in the MF-35 of 1959–1965. Displacement on the three-cylinder engine was 152.7 ci (2500 cc), and it provided 33.02 drawbar and 37.04 belt hp in Nebraska tests. Bore and stroke were $3\frac{5}{8}$x5 inches (91x125 mm), and its operating speed was up to 2,000 rpm.

A 60-hp MF-85 LPG was announced in 1959. Its 242-ci (3964-cc) Continental four was of $3\frac{7}{8}$x$5\frac{1}{8}$-inch (97x128-mm) bore and stroke, and developed 56.47 drawbar and 62.21 belt hp via an eight-speed transmission. A gas version had similar tests results. The MF-85 was made from 1959 to 1962.

In 1960, the MF-88 diesel arrived. It was nearly the same as the MF-85, but it was powered by a 276.5 ci (4520 cc) Continental four with 4x$5\frac{1}{2}$-inch (100x137.5-mm) bore and stroke. The MF-88's tests showed 55.54 drawbar and 63.31 belt hp.

Also new in 1960, the MF-65 diesel debuted with its 203.5-ci (3333-cc) four-cylinder Perkins diesel engine. It produced 42.96 drawbar and 48.59 belt hp in Nebraska tests, with it $3\frac{5}{8}$x5-inch (91x125-mm) engine running at up to 2,000 rpm via a six-speed transmission.

Massey-Ferguson bought Italian tractor maker Landini in 1960. Landini made only diesel-engined tractors from its beginning in 1910. M-F sold some of the blue-painted Landini models in the United States, and later manufactured some M-F models in Landini's Italian plants.

Looking to the Future

Meeting its competition with both large and small tractors kept Massey-Ferguson on its toes for the next twenty years. Massey losses began to mount in the late 1970s as interest rates soared and farm equipment sales lagged. Massey started selling divisions and consolidating production by closing plants. The early 1980s were financially brutal, and business conditions worsened.

In 1993, Massey-Ferguson's parent company, Varity Corporation, sold North American Massey-Ferguson distribution rights to Allis-Gleaner Company. AGCO was formed in 1990 to buy Deutz-Allis Corporation from its German owner, Klockner-Humboldt-Deutz. In 1994, Varity sold its Massey-Ferguson division as well to AGCO, but kept the Perkins engine operation. Today, Massey-Ferguson is still going strong under AGCO ownership.

1948 Massey-Harris Pony

Above: *Smallest of the Massey models was the diminuitive Pony. Like other small tractors of its day, the Pony was marketed to truck farms and to larger farms as a light-duty chore tractor. This 1948 model is in the collection of Jacob Dudkewitz of Cochranville, Pennsylvania. Both Jake and his son, Jay, collect and restore Masseys.*

1949 Ferguson TO-20

Left: *After the break from Ford, Irishman Harry Ferguson went it alone in the tractor business. Based largely on the Ford 2N, Ferguson's Model TO-20 was built in Detroit, Michigan, through the 1953 merger with Massey that created Massey-Harris-Ferguson.*

Minneapolis-Moline

*The Machine That Will Keep the
Boy on the Farm.*
—Minneapolis Universal Farm
Motor ad, 1910s

Above: **1935 Minneapolis-Moline Universal J**

1935 Minneapolis-Moline Universal J
Left: *The M-M Universal Model J had nearly as many uses as names. First introduced in 1934, the row-crop machine still carried the Twin City name on its radiator. The J was M-M's second-generation row-crop, and dispensed with the heavier design of the preceding Model Ms. This 1935 J was found and restored to its original gray and red by Dale Nafe of Pierson, Iowa.*

A rugged northern prairie flavor came through in the tractors produced by the new Minneapolis-Moline Power Implement Company after its organization in 1929. Three firms with long histories in making tractors and agricultural implements consolidated to form the new company. The parent firms were the Moline Implement Company of Moline, Illinois, the Minneapolis Steel & Machinery Company, and the Minneapolis Threshing Machine Company, both of the Minneapolis, Minnesota, area.

Moline Implement, formerly Moline Plow Company, contributed its broad line of plows, discs harrows, and other farm implements. Minneapolis Steel brought its Twin City tractor, and the Minneapolis Threshing firm contributed its Minneapolis combine, threshers, and corn shellers into the new company.

The Flying Dutchman

Moline Plow's predecessor company, Candee & Swan, was an early plow-making competitor of Deere. Candee & Swan and Deere struggled in court in 1867 over the right to call their product the Moline Plow. Deere won in district court, but the ruling was overturned by the Illinois Supreme Court in 1871, and Candee & Swan soon became the Moline Plow Company. After buying a sulky plow design in 1883 known as the Flying Dutchman, Moline Plow Company adopted the Flying Dutchman name and emblem as its trademark. Moline Plow discontinued use of the Flying Dutchman trademark at the onset of World War I.

By 1919, Moline Plow developed an advanced articulated general-purpose tractor called the Moline Universal with electric lights and starter. The end for the Universal came in 1923, during the tractor price wars instigated by Henry Ford and joined by International Harvester. All farm equipment makers were experiencing hard times in a post-WWI recession, and many of them stopped or paused production of some of their products.

The Twin City Tractor

Minnesota Steel and Machinery was organized in 1902 to build steel structures, but the company moved toward other types of manufacturing in 1903 with stationary steam engines and in 1904, with early gas engines. MS&M was soon contracting the manufacture of equipment for other firms, including Case Threshing Machine. In 1912, MS&M contracted to build 500 Case 30/60 tractors. The company also contracted in 1913 to build 4,600 Bull tractors, with Bull furnishing the en-

1920s Moline Universal advertisement

gines for the briefly popular three-wheeled machine.

MS&M also developed its own line of Twin City tractors in the meantime, and in 1915, it offered four different power sizes as the TC-15, TC-25, TC-40, and the monster TC-60. The company's 1913 Model 60/110 (later 60/90) had a six-cylinder engine with a 7¼x9-inch (181x225-mm) bore and stroke. The 60/90 was a ground shaker at nearly 14 tons (12,600 kg). By 1924, the company dropped the big tractors in favor of lighter tractors that gained popularity after World War I.

The TC 12/20 introduced in 1919 was a standard-configured tractor with a unit-frame construction. Four valves per cylinder—two intake and two exhaust with twin cams, no less!—was an innovation that improved the engine's breathing. Larger models followed, with a 20/35 in late 1919; the 17/28, an improvement on the 12/20, in 1924; a stronger tractor, the 27/44, was an improved 20/35, built from 1929 to 1935; and the 21/32 arrived in 1929.

The Minneapolis Tractor

Minneapolis Threshing Machine was a veteran producer of steam traction engines and threshing machines. The

1919 Moline Universal D

Above: *This 1919 Moline Universal Model D was an early general-purpose farm tractor. This last version, made from 1918 to 1923, came equipped with electric lights and a starter. The implement needed for each specific farm task, like the plow shown, attached under the seat, thus furnishing the rig's rear wheels. Jim Jonas of Wahoo, Nebraska, along with his father and his uncle, spent nine months restoring this historic tractor.*

1919 Moline Universal D controls

Left: *The steering wheel and other controls were placed near the operator via long rods.*

Above: **1915 Twin City 15 advertisement**

1924 Twin City 12/20

Right: *Smallest of the famed Twin City tractors from Minnesota Steel & Machinery was this 12/20-hp version. Its sixteen-valve four-cylinder engine is the first known on a farm tractor. The big cast-steel lugs weighed 10 lbs (4½ kg) each and were probably used in soft rice fields. Twin City experts say the wheels should be painted gray. This 1924 Model 12/20 was cut free from a large persimmon tree and put back into working order by Leslie Moffatt of Brighton, Tennessee.*

Eats Only When at Work.
—Minneapolis Universal Farm Motor
ad, 1910s

1937 Minneapolis-Moline ZTU
Not just streamlined, but Visionlined was the word from Minneapolis-Moline on its new 1937 Model ZTU row-crop. The Prairie Gold color and red noses were new, too. Virden Smith and his son, Biron, of Findlay, Ohio, made a family project out of restoring this 1937 ZTU.

company had a history that dated to 1874 and the Fond du Lac Threshing Machine Company of Fond du Lac, Wisconsin. In 1910, Minneapolis Threshing began to sell the Universal 20/40 two-cylinder opposed gas tractor made by the Universal Tractor Company of Stillwater, Minnesota.

MTM went on to develop its own line of gas tractors, including its 1911 Model 25/50 with a four-cylinder engine. Other MTM tractors were a 40/80 (later rated as a 35/70) in 1912, a 20/40 in 1914, and a 15/30 in 1915 (later designated a 12/25 after Nebraka tests).

Smaller models followed in the 1920s, including MTM's first tractor with a unit frame, the 1922 crossmounted four-cylinder 17/30. The MTM 17/30, with its radiator tank casting was identified as The Minneapolis tractor. Another interesting feature of the 17/30 was its belt idler pulley attached to the axle of its right front wheel. Two versions of the model were designated 17/30A and 17/30B.

The B version with its 4⅞x7-inch (122x175-mm) bore and stroke was a trend setter. The long-stroke concept from MTM, which gave an engine superior lugging power at low rpm, was passed on to the new Minneapolis-Moline designs of the 1930s. The long-stroke engine was kept alive by M-M as long as it made tractors; the engine design gave M-M tractors power to hang on and recover to governed speed on heavy loads, such as belt work for threshers and shellers.

Minnie-Mo on the Go

The new Minneapolis-Moline had a challenging task ahead in 1929. It needed to sell off old inventory from its three merged companies, and quickly develop new products for a rapidly changing market—all in the face of a deepening recession. M-M was up for the game.

First out in 1930 was the KT Kombination Tractor general-purpose machine. Designed with a bowed front axle and extra crop clearance, the two-plow 14/23 was a quadruple-duty machine, since it could cultivate two to three rows, pull tillage equipment, power belt applications, or run PTO-powered equipment. The 14/23 stayed in the M-M line through 1934, when it was upgraded as the KTA made until 1938. Orchard models were also built. The Twin City and M-M names were both cast in the radiator tops of the tractors from 1931 to about 1938; after that, only the M-M trademark appeared.

The first M-M tricycle row-crop was the Universal MT 13/25 introduced in 1931. The 4,860-lb (2,187-kg) machine was configured similar to the IH Farmall, with drop-box drive-wheel gearing to provide under-axle crop clearance. Front wheel steering was by way of a side rod turning the front wheels through a projecting lever, similar to the Case row-crop tractors. The 13/25's four-cylinder 4¼x5-inch (106x125-mm) engine was designed to run at up to 1,150 rpm. The MT was updated as the MTA in 1935, with an optional high-compression engine designed to burn 70-octane gas. Another option was a 10-mph (16-km/h) high-speed gear.

Goodby Rooster Roost

The M-M Universal J row-crop tractor introduced in 1935 used an F-head engine with exhaust valves in the block and intake valves in the head. M-M claimed the valves would be better cooled with the additional water jacketing surrounding them. The 3⅝x4¾-inch (91x119-mm) engine gave the J power for two plows. A five-speed transmission was in line with the times. In fifth gear, the J could scoot down the road at 12.2 mph (19.5 km/h)—if equipped with rubber tires. High-octane versions of the J were available in 1936, as were J orchard models.

The J resembled the earlier M, but its steering was via a worm-and-sector gear in the front pedestal, turned by a frame-mounted steering rod moving on ball bearings and connected to the angled steering column with a universal joint; its rooster roost was gone. The J's air cleaner, mounted on the steering pedestal, was a distinctive feature of the model.

Like other second-generation row-crop tractors, the J adopted large-diameter wheels attached to long axles driven directly from the differential. Hub clamps on the wheels allowed infinite wheel width adjustment. The Universal J was also made with standard tread.

Going Gold

Bright colors adorned farm tractors as makers pushed past the Great Depression and aimed at brighter times. The drab grays of the M-M tractors became history in 1937, when M-M's new Visionlined Model Z was introduced. An appropriately bright Prairie Gold color adorned the new streamlined machine. Neither yellow nor orange, the color lay somewhere in between and seemed to reflect the color and warmth of ripening wheat in late-summer sunshine. Picking up the red from the wheels of its previous tractors, M-M used the contrasting color on radiator grills and wheels to mark the line of tractors now affectionately called Red Noses by classic tractor buffs.

The tapered Visionlined hood of the Z gave its row-crop operator better visibility for cultivating. Also new on the Z was an engine design that permitted it to run on 70-octane gasoline or the cheaper fuels such as kerosene or distillates. A detachable cylinder head with adjustable protrusions in the combustion chamber permitted the compression ratio to be changed for either gas or low-cost fuels. The Zs were soon available as standard-tread models as well. The ZTU was a two-to-three-plow tractor that Nebraska tested at 20.98 drawbar and 27.95 belt hp in 1940. Its four-cylinder engine had $3\frac{5}{8}$x$4\frac{1}{2}$-inch (91x112.5-mm) bore and stroke and turned at up to 1,500 rpm.

The Famous Comfortractor

The 1938 M-M model introductions were big news. The beautiful new Prairie Gold three-to-four-plow Model U tractor enclosed in its futuristic all-weather cab with sweeping fenders was a crowd pleaser. The Model UDLX (for deluxe) had just about everything an operator might want. Its all-weather cab had roll-down side windows, full venting front windows with wipers, radio, top-mounted spotlight, jump seat for a passenger, heater, and even a horn. Electric lights, starter, foot accelerator, and five-speed transmission gave the machine added performance, too—up to 40 mph (64 km/h), if the road surface permitted. The UDLX became known as the Comfortractor.

But for all its gloss and appeal, the UDLX was not fully appreciated for nearly fifty years, until it became a favorite of classic tractor collectors. Only about 150 UDLXs were made between 1938 and 1941, and with, perhaps, only half of them surviving, UDLXs today can sell for close to twenty times their original new price.

Ironically, cost was the major stumbling block to the UDLX's original sales success. The added equipment nearly doubled the price of the same tractor without the frills. Under the skin it was a hefty tractor, and the UDLX saw use by their farm owners and custom combine operators who appreciated the model's speed and comfort in long pulls between jobs. Some rural mail carriers in the northern prairie states also praised the UDLX's snug warm cab and go-anywhere capability, when the north wind howled and the drifts were deep.

The Model U engines were four-cylinders of $4\frac{1}{4}$x5 inches (106x125 mm) bore and stroke, and helped the tractor deliver 30.86 drawbar and 38.12 belt hp at 1,275 rpm when tested at Nebraska in 1938. The U was available as a row-crop tricycle and in standard tread.

Another enclosed-cab tractor, M-M's two-plow tricycle-front row-crop Model R was available from 1939 to 1941. The R was less expensive than the U, but it did not sell well. Only about 400 Comfort-Cab-equipped Rs were sold. The RTU, tested at Nebraska in 1940, delivered 15.58 drawbar and 20.49 belt hp from its $3\frac{5}{8}$x$4\frac{1}{2}$-inch (91x112.5-mm) engine turning at 1,400 rpm. The cab-equipped R had a front-mounted two-row cultivator. The belt pulley could be used, but its clearance from the cab was minimal. In 1941, the two-plow R was available either in tricycle or standard-tread wheel configurations. It was to be another thirty years before fully enclosed cabs became popular on U.S. farm tractors.

Also new in 1939 was the M-M Model GT, a standard-tread- or wheatland-type tractor with four-to-five-plow power. The GT was tested by at Nebraska in 1939, and it produced 36.27 drawbar and 48.93 belt hp from by its four-cylinder $4\frac{5}{8}$x6-inch (116x150-mm) engine turning at 1,075 rpm.

LPG Pioneer

Liquified Petroleum Gas, a pressurized mixture of volatile petroleum waste gasses, including butane and propane, was bottled for fuel use in the mid-1930s. Experiments were underway for using LPG as engine fuel, and, in 1941, Minneapolis-Moline was the first tractor maker to offer factory-built LPG tractors. Other manufacturers soon followed, and LPG became an alternative to gas and kerosene or distillate for fuel. Down the road, diesel-fueled tractors would replace most LPG uses.

World War II interrupted model introductions at M-M, as it did the other tractor makers. Some of M-M's defense contracts were for utility towing vehicles based on tractor models. One of these, a four-wheel-drive unit based on the U Series, is said to have inspired the name "Jeep," later used as the name for the lightweight all-purpose military vehicle.

Restyling and upgrading of the Z, G, U, and R Series began about 1948. The 1948 ZA boasted a flat front with louvered grill painted Prairie Gold instead of the previous red. The 2A was available in a general-purpose row-crop version with twin front tricycle wheels as the ZAU, in a single-front-wheel version designated the ZAN, with adjustable wide-front and rear-tread width called the ZAE, and in a standard-tread version named the ZAS.

The big G was converted to burn LPG in 1950, and designated the GTC. The GTB gas version was produced from 1951 to 1953.

In 1949, the U was the first factory-designed LPG-burning tractor to be tested at Nebraska. The U model stayed in production from 1947 to 1959. The UTC high-clearance sugar-cane version was available 1948–1954.

The R Series was available with disc brakes, and it received the same styling change as the Z in the early 1950s. It, too, was available in different wheel configurations.

Uni-Tractor and Diesel Power

A universal power unit for propelling various harvesting equipment was developed by M-M in 1952. Called the Uni-Tractor Model L, the unit was designed to mount and power M-M's Uni-Forager, Uni-Harvestor, Uni-Picker/sheller, Uni-Baler, and other powered implements. Its nickname was the Motorcycle because its left front drive wheel, powertrain, and rear wheel lined up in a row with the operator seated top front. The right drive wheel was at the end of a long, reinforced axle housing where the accessory machine was mounted. The Uni-Tractor was originally powered by a 206-ci (3374-cc) V-4 engine that was replaced in 1960 with an inline engine of the same displacement. New Idea of Coldwater, Ohio, bought the Uni-Tractor and its equipment line in 1962.

Diesel power joined the M-M lineup in the mid-1950s. Largest of the diesel lot was the six-cylinder GB, turning out 55.44 drawbar and 62.78 belt hp in its Nebraska tests in 1955. It was produced between 1955 and 1959. Diesel engines also powered some U models.

The familiar hand clutch was missing on the new M-M Models 445 and 335 introduced in 1956. The new models also had live PTO, power steering, and three-point hitch with draft control. Travel speeds were doubled with a new Ampli-torc that allowed on-the-go shifting. The 335 was powered with a 165-ci (2703-cc) Minneapolis engine, and the tractor showed 29.84 drawbar and 33.5 belt hp in its Nebraska tests. The 335 stayed in the M-M line until 1961.

The M-M 5-Star replaced the UB in 1957. Its 283-ci (4636-cc) LPG engine developed 54.96 maximum hp in Nebraska tests, and the 336-ci (5504-cc) diesel version 54.68 maximum hp. The 5-Star was made from 1957 to 1961.

In 1959, M-M replaced the 455 with the 4-Star, available with 206-ci (3374-cc) gas, LPG, or diesel engines. The 4-Star had improved hydraulics and new styling. Tests of the gas 4-Star showed 44.57 maximum hp; the LPG version produced 45.45 maximum hp. The 335 was replaced with the Jet Star and was restyled. The GB replacement was the G-VI, and its six-cylinder 425.5-ci (6970-cc) LPG engine produced 78.44 maximum hp, compared with 78.49 hp for the diesel version.

The White Merger

In 1960, the M-5 model replaced the 5-Star. It was to be about the last model change at Minneapolis-Moline. Maximum test power from the M-5 diesel version was 58.15 hp from the 336-ci (5504-cc) engine running at 1,500 rpm. The M-5 was made between 1960 and 1963.

In 1963, White Motor Corporation acquired Minneapolis-Moline, and the M-M name disappeared. In 1962, White bought Cockshutt Farm Machinery of Brantford, Ontario, and the Oliver Corporation of Chicago. In 1969, the three companies merged into a new firm created by White called White Farm Equipment, a wholly owned subsidiary of White Motor Corporation.

1938 Minneapolis-Moline UDLX

Driving comfort and go-to-town luxury were promised by the 1938 UDLX Comfortractor. Obviously ahead of its time, tractor cabs weren't well accepted for another thirty years. A five-speed transmission gave the slick-looking UDLX a road speed of up to 40 mph (65 km/h). The tractor's lines are reminiscent of truck cab styles of the mid-1930s. A fold-out jump seat provided amenities for at least one additional passenger. Another version of the UDLX, a sports roadster with the fenders but not the cab, was also designed. Only about 150 UDLX tractors were sold. Don Kingen of McCordsville, Indiana, employed custom restoration work to return his UDLX to like-new shape. The blue ribbon won by the tractor at the 1988 Indiana State Fair hangs proudly from the rearview mirror.

1938 Minneapolis-Moline UTU

Above: *The 1938 M-M Model UTU was a brawny tractor. The UTU is the row-crop version of the machine that was the basis for the famous UDLX Comfortractor. Like the smaller M-M row-crop tractors, the UTU was Visionlined to help the operator better see the cultivating operation. This UTU is from the collection of Roger Mohr, a nationally known Minne-Mo specialist from Vail, Iowa.*

1949 Minneapolis-Moline ZAU

Right: *A new flat-styled grill adorns the front of the 1949 M-M Model ZAU rebuilt by James Garrod of Sheridan, Indiana. Garrod grew up with the tractor on his farm home in Michigan. The model was built from 1949 to 1952.*

You can help stabilize peace by stabilizing the economy of a nation.
—Minneapolis-Moline ad, 1949

1939 Minneapolis-Moline R with cab

Above: *Farm work was to be eased by the factory-built cab on the M-M Model R row-crop tractor of 1938, but the cab's extra cost and inconvenience spoiled its success. Nice for winter and cool springs, the cabs became ovens during the summer months, when most fields were cultivated. Alvin Egbert of New Bremen, Ohio, put this 1939 model back together.*

1939 Minneapolis-Moline R cab

Left: *The Model R cab gave the operator low vertical windows under the windshield to view rows being cultivated. The seatback folded down to aid entry and exit through the narrow rear door.*

Machinery will make your Farm a "Land of Freedom."
—Minneapolis-Moline wartime ad, 1941

Chapter 10

Oliver

Your fall plowing—is it done!!!
If not, buy a Hart-Parr Oil Tractor and
get it done at once.
—Hart-Parr ad, 1912

Above: **1951 Oliver 77 Orchard**

1937 Oliver Hart-Parr 70 Standard
Left: *This 1937 Oliver Hart-Parr 70 Standard was equipped with the same engine as the row-crop 70. Jon Clow of Centreville, Maryland, restored this tractor. His is on steel wheels, although many 70 Standards came on rubber.*

The pioneering tractor firm of Hart-Parr Company of Charles City, Iowa, was an essential part of the new Oliver Farm Equipment Corporation of Chicago, formed in 1929 by the merger of four historic farm-equipment makers. Joining Hart-Parr were Oliver Chilled Plow Company of South Bend, Indiana; Nichols & Shepard Company of Battle Creek, Michigan; and American Seeding Machine Company of Springfield, Ohio. The new company used the name of one of its constituent companies and the products and ideas of all four to build a successful new full-line farm-implement maker.

Oliver dated back to 1855 when its Scottish-born founder James Oliver invented the chilled steel plow. His patented process produced a plow with a hard surface and a tough core.

Nichols & Shepard had been building threshing machines since 1850, when John Nichols built his first threshing machine in the blacksmith shop he had operated since 1848. Nichols & Shepard was famous for its Red River Special threshing machines.

American Seeding Machine was formed in 1903 with the merger of five farm-equipment makers. Among its many products was the Superior grain drill.

At the time of the merger, full-line companies such as IH and Deere ruled the field. Not to combine and compete could quickly kill a firm. It happened with increasing frequency as the U.S. economy slowed to a crawl in the late 1920s. Mergers and acquisitions became frequent as firms faced a fiercely competitive future with drained capital resources

After the 1929 merger, Oliver's initial challenge was to develop a general-purpose row-crop tractor and update the aging Hart-Parr tractor line. The Hart-Parrs were developed at the turn of the century and improved over nearly thirty years of manufacture. But by the late 1920s, the Hart-Parrs were still chugging away as mostly two-cylinder designs with little promise of general-purpose use.

Charles and Charles in Charles City

Charles W. Hart and Charles H. Parr began their pioneering work on gas engines in the late 1800s while studying mechanical engineering at the University of Wisconsin at Madison. In 1897, the two men formed the Hart-Parr Gasoline Engine Company of Madison. In 1900, they moved their operation to Hart's hometown of Charles City, Iowa, where they found financing to make gas traction engines based on their innovative ideas.

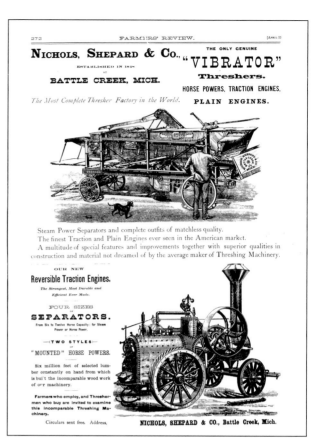

1890s Nichols, Shepard & Company advertisement
Above: *Oliver Farm Equipment was formed in 1929 by the merger of four historic farm-equipment makers, including Nichols, Shepard of Battle Creek, Michigan.*

1925 Hart-Parr 12/24
Facing page, top: *A force-feed Madison-Kipp oiler kept lubricants flowing to the two-cylinder Hart-Parr 12/24 of 1925. First introduced in 1924 by the Charles City, Iowa, tractor maker, this series soldiered on until replaced by the Oliver four-cylinder tractors after the firms joined in 1929. Lyle Spitznogle of Wapello, Iowa, owns this tractor.*

1929 Cockshut Hart-Parr 18/28
Facing page, bottom: *Cockshutt Plow Company of Brantford, Ontario, sold this product of the early Oliver company to the Canadian market. The 1929 Cockshutt 18/28 still carries the famous Hart-Parr name. Richard Brown of Harriston, Ontario, Canada, had this tractor refurbished for his collection.*

> *It is no longer good business to have a lot of money invested in horse-flesh . . . when you can buy a Hart-Parr "Little Devil" Tractor.*
> —Hart-Parr ad, 1910s

1930 Oliver Hart-Parr 28/44
The Oliver Hart-Parr 28/44 was a new model in 1930. Like its smaller sibling, the 28/44 was an all-new tractor with three speeds powered by a larger 4¾x6¼-inch (119x156-mm) engine. David Preuhs of Le Center, Minnesota, collected and restored this proud Oliver with the help of his son, Wayne.

Their efforts led them to erect the first factory in the United States dedicated to the production of gas traction engines. Hart-Parr is also credited with coining the word "tractor" for machines that previously had been called gas traction engines.

The firm's first tractor effort, Hart-Parr No. 1, was made in 1901. It was a big two-cylinder 17/30 machine boasting a bore and stroke of 9x13 inches (225x325 mm). Field testing in 1902 showed the No. 1's weaknesses, and in 1903, Hart Parr No. 2 appeared. The 2 was a more powerful machine, with a 22/45 rating. Hart-Parr No. 3, introduced in 1903, was an 18/30 two-cylinder machine with a 10x13-inch (250x325-mm) bore and stroke. And it worked!

In fact, one No. 3 worked hard for seventeen years

for George H. Mitchell who lived just south of Charles City on the Clarksville Road. Mitchell bought the tractor in August 1903 for $1,580, and used it until 1919. In 1924, Mitchell sold the No. 3 back to Hart-Parr, and the machine was used in historical advertising displays for Hart-Parr and Oliver. In 1960, Oliver gave the historic No. 3 to the Smithsonian Institution in Washington, D.C., where it was displayed until 1991. It was then loaned to Lake Farmpark museum at Kirtland, Ohio.

In weight, scale, and performance, the early Hart-Parr tractors resembled their steam-engine competitors—not unusual, since the company was focused on that market. The big machines' weight was measured in tons, and the 40/80 machine built from 1908 to 1914 topped out at 18 tons (16,200 kg). The 60/100 machine

1936 Oliver Hart-Parr 70

Above: *Rubber tires were widely accepted by 1937, when this Oliver 70 rolled off the lines in the Charles City, Iowa, Oliver plant. These tires are original to the tractor. Electric lights and starter made it a breeze to spark the quiet six-cylinder engine featured in this second-generation Oliver row-crop tractor. Jean L. Olson of Chatfield, Minnesota, has a special affinity for his 1936 Oliver 70: it is like the one he drove for years while farming.*

1937 Oliver 70 Standard

Left: *The rounded rear fenders on the Oliver 70 Standard were just a hint of the dramatic streamlining to come in the years following 1937.*

of 1911 to 1912 came out at a massive 26 tons (23,400 kg). Even the smaller-horsepower rigs weighed up to 10 tons (9,000 kg).

Lightweight Little Devil

The Hart Parr Little Devil of 1914–1916 was among the company's first tries at building a lighter tractor aimed at replacing horses on the farm. The Little Devil was of unusual design, including one centered rear drive wheel with two wheels in front. Its two-cylinder two-cycle engine was company-rated at 15/22 hp. Ads for the machine called it, "The tractor that fits every farm," and noted that it could be bought for the price of three or four horses. Some 725 were made, but the Little Devil apparently did not replace enough horses and was gone by 1916.

The "New Hart-Parr" of 1918 took better aim at the emerging lightweight tractor market. The 12/25 tractor employed a two-cylinder horizontal engine with 6½x7-inch (162.5x175-mm) bore and stroke and was of more conventional design. The 15/30 Type A of 1918–1922 was upgraded to the Type C in 1922 and to the Type E in 1924–1926. A smaller-engined 10/20, designated Model B, was produced in 1921; the 10/20 Model C of 1922–1924 had a slightly larger engine.

Four-cylinder power in the 22/40 and 28/50 was achieved by widening the tractor frames and basically fastening together two of the smaller, two-cylinder engines. All were horizontal low-speed engines; only after the 1929 Oliver merger were the tractor designs upgraded to vertical four-cylinder engines mounted lengthwise on the tractor frame.

Oliver Row-Crop Tip-Toes In

Oliver Chilled Plow engineers started work on a row-crop tractor after J. D. Oliver determined that Henry Ford did not plan to develop a row-crop design. By 1926, an Oliver prototype was at work in Texas, based on a design by Oliver Chilled Plow engineer Herman Altgelt. Altgelt is also credited with redesigning the wheels into the tip-toe configuration that handled the sticky gumbo at the Texas test site. Patent applications for the tractor were filed in 1928, and in that same year nine prototypes were tested. Each design had the name Oliver cast in the radiator, each was painted gray with red wheels, and each was designated either Model A for the tricycle row-crop or Model B for the standard-tread machines.

The 1929 formation of the Oliver Farm Equipment Sales Company changed everything, but the Oliver design was to shape the new firm's entry into the row-crop market. Oliver first used "floating" adjustable rear wheels on the prototype South Bend tractor, and other tractor makers soon followed. New engines, drivetrains, and transmissions were to transform the South Bend design into the Oliver row-crop machines produced starting in February 1930.

In 1930, the year after its founding, Oliver introduced its own row-crop tractor, a tricycle-type tractor with a single front wheel. Skeleton steel rear wheels had a narrow vertical band to which twenty spade lugs were alternately attached left then right, giving it "power on tip-toe," according to Oliver ads. The rear wheels were attached to the rear axles with a hub that could be loosened. That allowed the wheels to slide on the axle to the desired row spacing, an idea that came from the South Bend engineers. On Oliver row-crop tractors built from 1931 to 1937, the large single front wheel was replaced with two close-spaced smaller-diameter wheels.

The row-crop was powered by an 18/27 four-cylinder engine that was related to the engines in its new line of standard tractors. The row-crop's transmission was also from the standards.

Oliver Hart-Parr standard tractors for 1930 included the 18/28 Series available as Standard, Western, Ricefield, and Orchard versions, built until 1937. The 28/44 was built from 1930 to 1937 in versions with either four- or six-cylinder engines, later becoming the Oliver Model 90.

The Oliver Hart-Parr Row-Crop 70 HC, a streamlined high-compression gas six-cylinder row-crop on pneumatic tires, came out in October 1935. Its quiet, smooth-running engine attracted a lot of attention, and the tractor was immediately popular. Oliver sold 5,000 of the new model by February—some 3,000 more than expected. That success proved that high-test gas was a viable tractor fuel. A companion tractor that could burn kerosene or distillate, the Row-Crop 70 KD, was announced later that year. Starter and lights were available on both.

In 1937, Oliver dropped Hart-Parr from the tractor names when it debuted improved streamlined 70 Row-Crops. Nebraska tests in 1940 showed 22.64 drawbar and 28.37 belt hp from the high-octane Row-Crop's six-cylinder 3⅛x4⅝-inch (78x117-mm) engine at 1,500 rpm. The 70 was also available in Standard, Industrial, and Orchard versions, made from 1937 to 1948.

New in 1938 was the Model 80 Row-Crop tractor, a three-plow version of the 18/27. It, too, was available with either 70-octane or kerosene/distillate-burning engines. The KD (kerosene/distillate) tested 23.27 draw-

1939 Oliver 80
This hefty 1939 Oliver 80 Row Crop looks ready to pounce on the weeds with its forward-mounted adjustable wide front. Its big four-cylinder engine gave it three-plow power. Bill Meeker and his son, Sam, of North Henderson, Illinois, show their Oliver collection every chance they get.

bar and 35.14 belt hp in 1938 Nebraska tests. Its engine was a four-cylinder design of 4½x5¼-inch (112.5x131-mm) bore and stroke running at up to 1,200 rpm. In 1940, the Model 80 was offered in a diesel version with a Buda-Lanova engine; Oliver later made its own diesel engine.

Styling on the 80 apparently was not a principal consideration. The tractor carried the boxy look of Oliver's earlier tractors. Adjustable-tread-width-axle front ends were available for row-crop conditions where the extra stability was needed.

Oliver Standard tractors for 1937 included an improved 28/44 called the Model 90. It had an electric starter, pressure lubrication, and four-speed transmission. The Oliver 80 Standard was the new designation

for the old 18/28 Oliver Hart-Parr. Its high-octane gas engine produced 27.66 drawbar and 36.07 belt hp in 1940 Nebraska tests. The Oliver 80 Standard was powered by a 4¼x5¼-inch (106x131-mm) high-compression engine designed to run at up to 1,200 rpm. Oliver 90 and 99 Standards were made simultaneously from 1938 to 1952. The 90 had a kerosene engine, and the 99 had a gas engine. From 1953 to 1957, the 90 and 99 became simply the Model 99.

More Gears and More Go

Highlighting Oliver's 1940 introductions was a new small tractor, the 60 Row-Crop. It was a small, trim version of the popular 70 Row-Crop, and was powered by a four-cylinder 3⁵⁄₁₆x3½-inch (83x87.5-mm) engine.

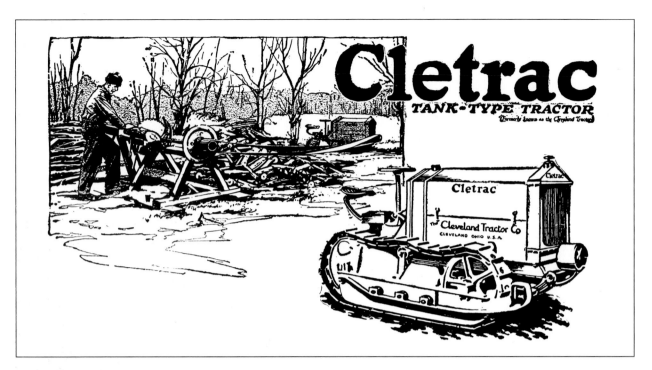

1920s Cletrac advertisement

The 60 weighed just 2,000 lb (900 kg) on rubber tires. Initially available with a four-speed transmission, the 60 got a five-speed gearbox in 1944. It was changed to battery ignition after production started in 1940.

Oliver also enhanced the 70 Row-Crop with a six-speed transmission, and upgraded the Standards to four-speeds. By this time, all of the Olivers had lights and starters.

Cletrac Crawlers

Oliver added another dimension to its line in 1944 when it took over the Cleveland Tractor Company of Cleveland, Ohio, and added the Cletrac line of farm crawlers to Oliver's Meadow Green-painted tractors. Oliver then shortened its name to the Oliver Corporation.

Cleveland Tractor traced its history back to 1911, when Rollin H. White, famous for his steam automobile and gas racing engines, and his brother Clarence White, developed a tracklayer tractor called the Cleveland Motor Plow. Unlike the Caterpillar tractors of its day, the Motor Plow used differential steering. Brake bands actuated by a steering wheel slowed one track and speeded up the other to turn the machine. Cat tractors used two lever-operated steering clutches to slow or stop one track and let the other continue to make a turn.

Cleveland Motor Plow Company was incorporated in 1916, and produced its first tractor, the Model R with 10 drawbar hp. The ads of the days said the Motor Plow

was "Geared to the Ground." The company name was changed to Cleveland Tractor in 1917, and the trademark Cletrac was adopted in 1918. Following models included the H 12/20 of 1918, the W 12/20 of 1920, and the smaller F 9/16 of 1921. Some forty different Cletrac models were made between 1917 and 1944, when it was sold to Oliver.

Cletrac's Model 80 of 1933 was its first diesel. A smaller diesel, the 35, was available in 1934. Row-crop farming was addressed in the 1935 Model E, which came in five tread widths from 31 to 76 inches (77.5 to 190 cm). The three-to-four-plow Model E could cultivate four rows with a front-mounted cultivator. A more compact model, the HG, came out in 1939. It, too, was available in different tread widths to accommodate row-cropping applications.

The first and only Cletrac wheel-type tractor, the GG or General, was built from 1938 to 1941. The General was a tricycle row-crop machine with a single front wheel. It was powered by a Hercules four-cylinder 3x4-inch (75x100-mm) engine. Power output at Nebraska was 14.26 drawbar and 19.29 belt hp. The General was sold by the B. F. Avery Company of Louisville, Kentucky, after 1941 and eventually ended up as part of the Minneapolis-Moline product line. Oliver did not need the General since it had its own small row-crop tractor.

Oliver restyled Cletrac's HG crawler in 1947, painted it Meadow Green, and offered it for farm use in four

1939 Cletrac E-62

Above: *Five years before it became part of Oliver, the Cleveland Tractor Company of Cleveland, Ohio, made this 1939 E-62. Owner Wilbur Lutz of Sinking Spring, Pennsylvania, says the figure in the model designation refers to track spacing of 62 inches (155 cm) for row-crop uses.*

1939 Cletrac E-62

Left: *Optional Cletrac equipment included a belt pulley and PTO. Grousers could be removed from the tracks for use in potato fields. An electrical system with starter and lights added to the Cletrac's daily utility.*

tread widths of 31 inches, 42 inches, 60 inches, and 68 inches (77.5 cm, 105 cm, 150 cm, and 170 cm). The HG's four-cylinder engine developed 18 drawbar and 22 belt hp.

A rubber-belted version of the HG, the HGR, was given a field trial in 1947, after several preproduction units were assembled. The gas tractor was a standard HG, but it incorporated a continuous belt-type "rubber band" in place of the steel tracks. The lower track-wheel design of the HGR resembled the military bogey wheel used on tanks.

The innovative rubber-belt crawler was not a success, as noted by Oliver Equipment Sales Engineer C. C. Colby in a 1946 letter describing the trials. Test engineers reported that more of the rubber track stayed on the ground over uneven terrain. Yet, although the rubber track had merit, it was difficult to keep it properly tensioned since it stretched when used and the rubber compounds did not hold up well. Work was stopped, and it was forty years before the rubber-belt concept was used again. This time it was used by Caterpillar on its Challenger farm crawlers of 1987.

Live PTO in the Fleetline Fleet

John Nichols of Nichols & Shepard (one of the founding firms of Oliver) started his company in 1848. In 1948, a new line of tractors was announced to celebrate Oliver's centennial.

The Fleetline tractors with new grill and sheetmetal styling included the Models 66, 77, and 88. They were all equipped with independent, or live, PTO, the first wheel-type tractors in the United States to be so equipped. Oliver introduced live PTO in 1946, an industry first. This feature permitted a PTO-driven machine to run whether the tractor was in motion or at rest.

The one-to-two-plow Model 66 came with three engine choices: a 129-ci (2113-cc) high-compression gas or diesel engine, or a 145-ci (2375-cc) lower-compression kerosene/distillate engine. Oliver also offered kerosene/distillate engines of larger displacement but lower compression in the 77 and 88. The two-to-three-plow Model 77 offered the six-cylinder 194-ci (3178-cc) engine in either gas or diesel versions. The three-to-four-plow Model 88 came with a six-cylinder engine of 231 ci (3784 cc) as either gas or diesel. Standard-tread and adjustable-wide-front versions were offered in the 66, 77, and 88 models; Orchard models were also made.

A new Oliver compact utility-type tractor, the Super 55, was announced in 1954. It was available with gas or diesel engines and featured a three-point hitch with draft control. The trend toward compact utility tractors began with the Ford-Ferguson 9N of 1939. In its type, the operator sat low, slightly forward of the rear axle, and straddled the transmission on a seat mounted above the differential. The Super 55 gas engine delivered 29.6 drawbar and 34.39 belt hp.

The Super Series also included the Super 66, Super 77, and Super 88, all with more power. The Supers were made from 1954 to 1958, with additional Supers debuting in 1957. The Super 44 was a new smaller utility-type tractor with the engine and drivetrain offset to the left to permit better under-tractor and forward vision for cultivating with the one-row machine. The Super 44's power came from a 139.6-ci (2287-cc) four-cylinder Continental L-head engine.

The Super 99 diesel of 1954 replaced the older 99 with two diesel engines available. The six-cylinder Oliver diesel was supplemented by a supercharged three-cylinder two-cycle General Motors diesel. Optional equipment included a torque-converter transmission and all-weather cab. The Nebraska test recorded 73.31 drawbar and 78.74 belt hp from the blower-equipped GM-engined version.

In 1958, the Oliver tractor line was given new radiator grill styling with bold horizontal stripes. The Meadow Green machines were accented by Clover White wheels

1939 Cletrac General GG

Facing page, top: *Cletrac's only wheel-type tractor was its small General, or Model GG. The General's engine was a Hercules 3x4-inch (75x100-mm) four-cylinder, working through a three-speed transmission. Owner William G. Menke, III, of Mentor, Ohio, put this 1939 General back together from a pile of parts.*

Montgomery Ward sold the General during the early 1940s. The General didn't follow Cletrac to Oliver in 1944, but was sold to B. F. Avery of Louisville, Kentucky. There it became the foundation for the firm's light tractor line. B. F. Avery later became part of Minneapolis-Moline.

1940 Oliver 80 Diesel

Facing page, bottom: *Oliver specialist Lyle Dumont of Sigourney, Iowa, owns this rare 1940 Oliver Diesel Row Crop. This machine has the Buda-Lanova engine that Oliver later replaced with its own diesel. Only about seventy-five tractors were made using the Buda-Lanova diesel.*

1948 Co-Op E3

It looks like a Cockshutt and runs like a Cockshutt, but it's a Co-Op Model E3. Cockshutt made this 1948 Co-Op E3 for sale by The National Farm Machinery Cooperative, Inc., of Bellevue, Ohio. Other than the color, the E3 is exactly the same as the Cockshutt Model 30. Fittingly, it is owned by another cooperative, Midland Co-Op, Inc., of Stilesville, Indiana. Midland manager Sid Bryan and plant employee Dave Frayser did the restoration.

and grills. Model numbers became 440, 550, 660, 770, 880, and 990. Also available were Models 950 and 995. The Oliver 995 GM Lugmatic diesel had an automatic torque converter. More power and an improved power transmission were featured. Full-time power steering became standard.

Bigger changes for Oliver came in 1960, after introductions of new models with the square-section eggcrate grills. New were the 500, with a David Brown engine, and the 1800 and 1900 Models.

Oliver Swallowed Whole

In November 1960, the White Motor Corporation of Cleveland, Ohio, bought Oliver. White followed with the purchase of Cockshutt in 1962 and Minneapolis-Moline

in 1963. The products from these acquisitions were gradually merged in the intervening years, and in 1969, these three divisions were re-assembled as White Farm Equipment, a wholly owned subsidiary of the White Motor Corporation.

TIC Investment Corporation of Dallas, Texas, bought White Farm Equipment in 1981 and continued its operation as WFE. Hard economic times caused WFE to file for bankruptcy in 1985. Allied Products Corporation of Chicago bought parts of WFE at that time, including the tractor factory in Charles City, Iowa, and all tooling and inventory. By 1987, Allied had combined its White Farm Equipment with its New Idea companies into a new division called White-New Idea. In 1993, AGCO bought the White-New Idea implement line.

1950 Oliver HG 68

Above: *Robert Tallman of Harbeson, Delaware, is a retired Oliver dealer who still loves the old machines he once sold and serviced. His 1950 Oliver Cletrac HG 68 sparkles with the care he has endowed on it to bring it back to life. Potato farmers used the machines with the 68-inch (170-cm) tread to straddle two 34-inch (85-cm) rows. The crawler's light footprint prevented compaction.*

1947 Oliver HGR with rubber treads

Left: *"Rubberband" tracks were experimental on a few Oliver HGRs in 1947. Rubber compounds apparently were not up to today's standards, as the trial was stopped. This tractor was displayed at the 1995 Ageless Iron Expo at Ankeny, Iowa, by Harlan Thompson of Harper, Kansas.*

Sturdy is the word for Oliver.
—Oliver 70 ad, 1941

1951 Oliver 77 Orchard
Above: *In 1948, the Oliver Fleetline Models 66, 77, and 88 replaced the Models 60, 70, and 80, and lasted in production until 1954. This 1951 Oliver 77 Orchard is owned by Verlan Heberer of Belleville, Illinois.*

1951 Oliver 77 Orchard controls
Right: *The instrument panel gauges are tucked under the operator's shielding. Perforations in the shield pass light for daytime visibility.*

1951 Cockshutt 30 Diesel
Above: *Although not a part of Oliver until 1962, Cockshutt did cooperate with Oliver on mutually beneficial projects for many years. Jeff Gravert, Cockshutt restoration specialist from Central City, Nebraska, restored this Model 30 and added his own finishing touch: the sparkling chrome exhaust stack.*

1951 Cockshutt 30 Diesel with umbrella
Left: *The single front tire available on the Model 30 tractor was ideal for cultivating bedded crops and flood-irrigated fields. The umbrella blocked the sun, but not the breeze.*

Chapter 11

The Orphan Tractors

Every man who owns a Happy Farmer
Tractor boosts for it.
—LaCrosse Happy Farmer ad, 1910s

Above: **1915 Russell 30/60**

1910 Pioneer 30/60
Left: *The drive wheels on this Pioneer 30 are 8 feet (240 cm)*
in diameter and have rim extensions 3 feet (90 cm) wide. The
enclosed cab gave prairie operators a respite from the fierce
prairie storms often encountered on their long field rounds.
Irvin King of Artesian, South Dakota, restored this monster.

From the hundreds of manufacturers and inventors active in the farm tractor business between 1900 and 1960, less than a dozen survived into the 1960s. Some makers were fortunate enough to be bought out or merged into other companies. Some, once successful and famous as steam traction engine and threshing machine makers, didn't make the transition to gasoline power fast enough to compete and continue. These makes are lovingly referred to by collectors as the Orphans.

By about 1915, swirling changes in farm power swept many makers into oblivion. The writing was on the wall: the steam engine was doomed by the newfangled gas-powered tractor. By 1925, steam machines were as old as yesterday, and gas tractors were the rage. They were quickly becoming agile, all-around machines capable of handling almost any farm power task.

Recurring economic recessions and depressions also took their toll. Some makers with successful products fell on hard times and had to throw in the towel when receivables soared. A combination of liberal credit terms and hard times on the farm did in many makers.

Here are some tractors that live on only in fast-fading memories or as restored examples that pay homage to their contribution to farm mechanization in their day.

Avery Company

The Avery Company of Peoria, Illinois, was a well-known power in farm steam engines and threshing equipment. Its famous Undermounted steam engine faced formidable competition from the on-coming gasoline-engined machines, so Avery began its defense by building a gas tractor-truck in 1909. The model looked more like a truck than a tractor, but it was designed to do dual duty with round wooden plugs that made up the tread on the machine's wheels. The tractor-truck was discontinued in 1914.

About the same time, Avery built a huge one-cylinder 12x18-inch (300x450-mm) engine with a potential output of 65 hp. Demonstrated at the 1910 Winnipeg trials, the tractor was withdrawn halfway through the trials because of its poor showing.

Following that shaky entry into the tractor market, Avery moved forcefully into the gas tractor business, introducing more than one model each year between 1911 and 1924. Avery spawned a stable of light cultivating tractors between 1916 and the early 1920s to try to expand its market share. In moving up from its one-row four-cylinder 5/10 cultivating tractor to a two-row unit, Avery added two-cylinders to the engine to make

its more powerful six-cylinder Model C. By 1919, Avery was making eight gas-powered models ranging in power from a 5/10 unit up to its giant 40/80 (later re-designated the 45/65 following its Nebraska tests). Avery also developed and tested a four-cylinder 15/25 "Track Runner" front-wheeled crawler in 1923. In 1924, Avery filed for bankruptcy.

Reorganized as the Avery Power Machinery Company, the new company succeeded in keeping the wolf away from its doors until 1931, when it again went under. After another reorganization, Avery produced the Ro-Trak tractor in the late 1930s, an innovative effort that promised the benefits of a row-crop machine and the stability of a standard-tread tractor. That machine was Avery's last.

A. D. Baker Company

Prominent and respected steam-engine maker A. D. Baker Company of Swanton, Ohio, was one pioneer who sought to keep farm steam engines competitive with gas tractors by designing lightweight and more efficient steam engines. The Baker Company built steam engines from 1898 until about 1925, when it acknowledged the end of steam and changed over to gas-powered machines.

The first Baker gas tractor was its 22/40. Using mostly off-the-shelf components from other manufacturers, Baker had its husky 25/50 model ready by late 1927. When tested at Nebraska in 1929, the 25/50 delivered a surprising 43 drawbar and 67 belt hp. So, unlike many other tractors tested, the big Baker was redesignated a bigger 43/67, compared with the original designation of 25/50. Baker tractor production ended during World War II.

Robert Bell Imperial

Seaforth, Ontario was the home of Robert Bell Engine & Thresher Company, which sold and serviced the 22/40 Imperial Super-Drive, apparently made by the Illinois Tractor Company of Bloomington, Illinois. Illinois first offered its Illinois Super Drive in 1919. As the Illinois Silo Company, the firm began making light cultivating tractors in 1916. Its first larger tractor was the Illinois 12/30 of 1918.

Eagle Manufacturing

Eagle Manufacturing Company of Appleton, Wisconsin, made a variety of gas-powered farm tractors, beginning with a 1906 machine driven by a two-cylinder

1919 Avery 14/28

Above: *It looked rough, but it worked. The Avery Company of Peoria, Illinois, built a stable of early gas tractors when it realized steam was out. Tractor exhaust venting through the vertical tube radiator helped cool the engine. This 1919 Avery 14/28 shows its steam heritage in its wheels, gearing, and cooling. Kenneth Lage of Wilton, Iowa, keeps the four-cylinder horizontally opposed engine tuned and running.*

What Avery lacked in styling on its tractors, it made up for with pinstriping. Kenneth Lage's 14/28 could pull a three-bottom plow, and tipped the scales at 7,540 lb (3,400 kg). This model was built at Peoria, Illinois, from 1919 to 1921. The barn in the background is nearly as old as the tractor.

1930 Baker 25/50

Left: *The big 1930 25/50 Baker was one of the few tractors to return from its Nebraska tests with a bigger power rating than it had before it left. Nebraska engineers found the Baker turned out a surprising 43/67 hp. Owner Darius Harms of St. Joseph, Illinois, likes the big machine. A previous owner must have thought well of it, too. In 1938, the tractors went back to the factory in Swanton, Ohio, to be updated with rubber tires, a generator, and starter.*

The cards are just being dealt in the tractor game, and some of the big hands are as likely to fall outside as to fall inside the farm-implement industry.
—Barton W. Currie, *The Tractor*, 1916

1938 Avery Ro-Trak
Avery came back in 1938 with its last hope for success, a row-crop tractor. The 1938 Avery Ro-Trak sought the middle ground: a convertible front-tread tractor that could be a wide-front or a tricycle-type, depending on the need. The Ro-Trak was a two-plow tractor run by a six-cylinder Hercules engine. James Layton of Federalsburg, Maryland, put this tractor together from "chunks and pieces."

horizontally opposed engine. A 1911 model of 56 hp employed a four-cylinder engine. By 1916, Eagle sold 8/16- and 16/30-sized tractors and progressed through the 1920s with a series of two-cylinder machines.

In 1930, Eagle jumped from a horizontal two-cylinder tractor to a vertical six-cylinder engine powering its 6A Eagle. The 6A Eagle was a three-to-four-plow tractor equipped with the Waukesha 4x4¾-inch (100x119-mm) engine, giving it a 22/37 rating.

The Eagle line was complemented in the following years by a Model 6B row-crop and a 6C utility version, both powered with Hercules sixes of 3¼x4⅛ inches (81x103 mm). The uncertainties of World War II also doomed the Eagle tractors.

Sears Roebuck's Graham-Bradley
With lines and speed suggestive of its automotive heritage, the six-cylinder Graham-Bradley 20/30 tractor built by Graham-Paige Motors Corporation of Detroit, Michigan, was a hit from its introduction in 1938. Initially, the Graham-Bradley was marketed through mail-order giant Sears Roebuck & Co. of Chicago, Illinois, through Sears retail stores or catalog.

The Graham-Paige company had built a reputation on its high-performance vehicles and its race cars. With a high road gear capable of speeds up to 20 mph (32 km/h), the racy tractor took advantage of the technology of the times and came standard from the factory with starter and lights, rubber tires, PTO, and hydraulic lift.

Both row-crop and standard-tread versions of the Graham-Bradley were built during its relatively short life. By 1941, production had ceased. After World War II, plans were announced to produce the tractor again. Those plans were shelved, however, when Graham-Paige president Joseph Frazer merged the company with Henry

1922 Imperial Super Drive 22/40

The 1922 Imperial Super Drive is a treasure of the Ron MacGregor family of Kippen, Ontario. Ron's father bought the 22/40-hp tractor new in 1922 for $3,200 from the Robert Bell Engine & Thresher Company in nearby Seaforth, Ontario. The Illinois Tractor Company of Bloomington, Illinois, apparently sold its Illinois Super Drive to the Canadian firm for Canadian distribution.

J. Kaiser's interests and made the postwar automobiles—the Frazer, Kaiser, and the smaller car, the Henry J.

General Motors as Tractor Maker

In an effort to compete with Henry Ford's announced intention to build a lightweight tractor, General Motors of Pontiac, Michigan, researched many firms and, in 1918, bought the Samson Tractor Works of Stockton, California, manufacturer of the Samson Sieve-Grip tractor. GM subsequently bought a manufacturing plant at Janesville, Wisconsin, and expanded it to produce its Samson tractors, a model designed to compete with Ford's recently introduced Fordson.

The Samson Sieve-Grip was re-engined with a GMC truck motor and introduced in 1918. Priced at $1,750, the Sieve-Grip couldn't compete with the Fordson.

The Samson Model M was a Fordson look-alike that was designed and positioned to challenge the Fordson.

It came out in late 1918 at $650 per unit, and was apparently on target.

GMC announced another tractor, the Model D Iron Horse at about the same time as the M. GM bought the Iron Horse design, which was originally called the Jim Dandy motor cultivator. The small four-wheel-drive machine worked something like today's skid-steer loaders. Belts with idler tensioners served as clutches for each side of the machine. With both belts tightened, the machine moved straight ahead. Weighted levers were lifted to loosen both drive belts to stop. Loosening the right belt resulted in a right turn; loosening the left caused a left turn.

The tractor could be operated from its seat, or driven like a team. Reins attached through pulleys mounted above the levers allowed the machine to be controlled by an operator walking behind the machine. A tug to the left rein turned the machine that way; a tug to the

1932 Eagle 6A

Facing page, top: *Rated at 22/37 hp, the new Eagle 6 of 1930 was a big leap for Eagle Manufacturing of Appleton, Wisconsin, as the firm had previously made only two-lungers. Robert Brennan of Emmett, Michigan, rescued his 1932 6A from an Ohio barn where it was slowly sinking into the dirt. The Eagle 6A could pull three to four plows in its day.*

1918 Samson Sieve-Grip

Facing page, bottom: *Veteran collector Fred Heidrick of Woodland, California, owns this link to General Motors' short time in the farm-tractor business. His 1918 Samson Sieve-Grip was developed by GM from machines designed by the Samson Tractor Works of Stockton, California, a company GM purchased. This low-built, heavy machine did not sell well against the Fordson, and it was not available after 1919.*

The unusual design of the Sieve-Grip wheels gave the model its name. Mud is supposed to work through the holes in the big wheel castings and not plug them. The arrow at the tractor's front shows the driver which way the front wheel is pointing. Low steering gear and seat position suggest the tractor was designed for orchard and vineyard work. Oil cans hold lubricating oil and gas for priming the engine.

1919 Samson M

Above: *To sharpen its aim on the Fordson, GM brought out the Samson Model M in December 1918. The Samson even looked a bit like the Fordson, as you can see on this M, owned by Randall Knipmeyer of Higginsville, Missouri. The gap between the radiator and the gas tank was a Model M feature. By adding fenders, governor, belt pulley, and other items that were extra on the Fordson, GM had a viable product.*

Above: **1939 Sears Roebuck catalog advertisement for the Graham-Bradley**

1938 Graham-Bradley

Right: *Mail-order giant Sears Roebuck and Co. sold Graham-Bradley farm tractors through its big catalog and in its farm centers. Not only did the Graham-Bradley look fast with its sweeping lines and pointed nose, it was fast—up to a 20-mph (32-km/h) top speed. Made by auto builder Graham-Paige, the tractor was powered by the firm's own six-cylinder 3¼x4⅜-inch (81x109-mm) engine. Tests proved it as a 20/28-hp tractor, and its features helped set the pattern for tractors of its day. This 1938 Graham-Bradley is owned by Vern Anderson of Lincoln, Nebraska.*

right and the machine turned right. Pull on both reins and the tractor stopped. Pull harder on the reins and the tractor reversed as long as the reins were held back.

Although the Iron Horse was attractively priced at $450, the motor cultivator, of any make, was never a roaring success. Although the Samson M was marginally profitable, the entire tractor venture was not, and GM sustained heavy losses in the new enterprise. The post-World War I economy was poor and competition was fierce. GM dropped farm tractor production like a hot potato in 1922, and has not competed in the arena since.

Huber Manufacturing

With a farm equipment history tracing back to Civil War times, the Huber Manufacturing Company of Marion, Ohio, was already a veteran steam engine and thresher manufacturer in 1898. That year, the company bought the patent rights to the Van Duzen gas engine—the engine that had powered John Froelich's famous 1892 tractor. Huber made thirty tractors with the single-cylinder Van Duzen engine, but apparently took a hiatus from tractor production after that.

Huber returned in 1911 with tractors powered by two-cylinder horizontally opposed engines. Huber's Farmer's Tractor was expanded to two models by 1912. Also joining the model lineup in 1912 was a 30/60 four-cylinder heavyweight.

Crossmounted four-cylinder engines showed up in 1917 on the Huber Light Four of 12/25. The popular machine was built until 1928. A Super Four of 14/30 rating was announced in 1921. By 1925, its final year of production, it had grown to a 18/36 rating. An enclosed drivetrain with its crossmount four was a feature of the Master Four of 1922. The tractor was rated at 25/50. As modern as it was, the Master Four was replaced with more modern designs.

Vertical four-cylinder inline engines marked the series of Huber tractors starting in 1926. The Super Four 18/36 had a Stearns overhead-valve engine that was upgraded to a 21/39 rating in 1929. The Huber 20/40 of 1927 also was powered by a Stearns ohv motor. Its rating was upped to 32/45 after good grades at its 1929 Nebraska tests. The Model HK stayed in production until World War II. The bigger 25/50 of 1927 vintage got its rating bumped up by the its Nebraska tests that same year. The 25/50 came out of the tests with a 50/69 hp performance, so it was rerated conservatively as a 40/62 tractor. Its Stearns motor was of 5½x6½ inches (137.5x162.5 mm) bore and stroke.

Huber addressed its need for a row-crop tractor with the standard-tread 1931 Modern Farmer, which was equipped with an arched front axle and drop-box gearing on the rear axles to give it more crop clearance. A Light Four model of 1929 was a 20/36-rated tractor tested at Nebraska in 1929. Unlike the Super Fours and their Stearns powerplants, the Light Four was equipped with a Waukesha 4¾x6½-inch (119x162.5-mm) four-cylinder engine with a Ricardo head that promised prolonged fuel turbulence in the cylinder for better power and performance.

A Modern Farmer Model L (standard) and LC (tricycle row-crop) were announced in 1937 and produced until World War II. They were of about 27/43 hp rating on rubber. The L and LC's power was from a 4½x5½-inch (112.5x137.5-mm) Waukesha VIK engine. Both models were available with electric lights and starters. The Model B of 1937 was a streamlined row-crop of tricycle configuration powered with a Buda engine creating 27.5 brake hp. An orchard version was also available. Huber tractor production ended in 1941, but the company continues to produce construction equipment.

Pioneer of the Prairies

Winona, Minnesota, was home of Pioneer Tractor Manufacturing Company, the company that began making tractors in 1910 with the introduction of the Pioneer 30. The big machine stayed in its Pioneer line until 1927. The Pioneer 30 was driven by a 7x8-inch (175x200-mm) four-cylinder horizontally opposed engine, working through a three-speed transmission, giving it speeds up to 6 mph (10 km/h).

A small Model 15 was also available, as was a gargantuan 45/90 with a six-cylinder engine and 9-foot-diameter (270-cm) drive wheels. In 1916, a 15/30 Pony Pioneer with one drive wheel was offered. The company's 1917 Pioneer Special, also of a 15/30 rating, had its weight pared back to 8,500 lb (3,825 kg), compared with 24,000 lb (10,800 kg) for the Model 30.

A more conventional tractor replaced the Special in 1919, an 18/36-rated machine of only 6,000 lb (2,700 kg). It retained the four-cylinder horizontally opposed engine design used in the earlier tractors. After 1927, Pioneer does not appear in tractor listings.

Russell Builds Giants

Adapting a three-cylinder English design, Russell & Company of Massillon, Ohio, began its transition from steam engines and threshing machines to gas tractors in 1909. The Russell American 20/40 was built from 1909

1915 Russell 30/60

Above: *This 1915 Russell 30/60 was built in Massillon, Ohio, by Russell & Company. The firm's products had earlier included threshing machines and steam engines. Victor Duraj helped restore the cross-engined behemoth, and the big gas tractor is part of the antique tractor collection of the University of California at Davis.*

l915 Russell 30/60 flywheel

Left: *The big fan and tubular radiator were needed to cool the monstrous four-cylinder 8x10-inch (200x250-cm) engine.*

until 1914. A three-wheeled 30/60 with a cross-mounted four-cylinder engine introduced in 1911 was later called the Giant. In 1913, the Giant became a four-wheeled tractor rated at 40/80. It was built between 1914 and 1921, but after Nebraska testing the tractor became the 30/60, and stayed in production until 1927.

Russell made lighter tractors beginning in 1915 with its 12/24 Russell Jr. The later tractors were of standard-tread design with four-cylinder inline engines. Russell's 1917 Little Boss was rated 15/30. The company was sold in 1927 ending manufacture, although Russell tractors were serviced through 1942.

Silver Kings from Ohio

From a manufacturer of railroad locomotives came one of the fastest tractors of the 1930s. Fate-Root-Heath Company of Plymouth, Ohio, made its first tractor in 1933, the Plymouth 10/20. Equipped with rubber tires, the little machine could travel up to 25 mph (40 km/h) on the highway. By 1935, the F-R-H tractor line was painted silver and renamed the Silver King. Tricycle versions with a forward mounted single wheel appeared in 1936. The tricycle Silver Kings were row-crop ready, with cultivator mounts and added rear-axle clearance.

Right, top: **1941 Silver King advertisement**

1940 Silver King
Right, bottom: *The square hole in the front casting is the cultivator mount on this tractor. Streamlining in the form of a large-pointed radiator screen makes the 1940 model appear less disjointed than earlier models.*

1936 Silver King R-66
Facing page, top: *The Silver King tractors of the 1930s could outrun most tractors on the road. They were built by Fate-Root-Heath of Plymouth, Ohio. Owner Paul Brecheisen of Helena, Ohio, restored this 1936 Model R-66. The model numbers refer to the rear tire tread width of 66 inches (165 cm).*

1940 Silver King
Facing page, bottom: *By 1940, the Silver King had taken on some new lines—and more speed. The later models could run down the road at about 30 mph (48 km/h). A six-volt electrical system with starter and lights modernized the 1940 Silver King. Fenders enhanced operator safety by providing shielding from the tires. Perry Jennings of Decatur, Tennessee, got his 1940 model moving again with major work that started with freeing the stuck pistons.*

182

15 *Pioneer* Special 30

Above: **1910 Pioneer Special 15/30 advertisement**

1910 Pioneer 30/60

Left: *Irvin King of Artesian, South Dakota, put this enormous 1910 Pioneer 30 back on its wheels after it had rested for fifty-five years on the edge of a field. Finding the wheels was the real trick. The spokes had been cut from the wheels, and they were lying flat in a pasture as bull-proof watering tanks. King's restoration efforts netted him a snorting, rumbling, red monster weighing 12 tons (10,800 kg). Its four-cylinder horizontally opposed engine measures an equally gigantic 7x8 inches (175x200 mm) bore and stroke. King's Pioneer produces 60 hp on the belt pulley. Engine balance is so good, a nickel still stays balanced on edge while the motor runs—just like Pioneer's original ads claimed.*

An abundance of economical power.
—Pioneer 15/30 ad, 1910s

185

1918 Wisconsin 22/40
This 1918 Wisconsin 22/40 was made by the Wisconsin Farm Tractor Company of Sauk City, Wisconsin. Only about 600 tractors were made by the firm between 1917 and 1923. Owner Frank Wurth of Freeburg, Illinois, bought this Wisconsin 22/40 from its original owner in 1977. Wurth's Wisconsin is powered by a four-cylinder Beaver engine.

Row-crop models were designated by numbers referring to rear wheel spacing in inches, including 60 inches, 66 inches, and 72 inches (150 cm, 165 cm, and 180 cm).

In 1940, the model designations were increased to three numbers, the first two still indicating rear-tire tread width. The new models also ran faster by 5 mph, up to 30 mph (8 km/h faster up to 48 km/h).

By 1956, manufacture of the Silver King tractor moved to West Virginia where it was made by Mountain State Fabricating Company of Clarksburg. Silver King production stopped in the late 1950s.

Wisconsin from Wisconsin

Earl McFarland and John Westmount started their tractor company in Sauk City, Wisconsin, in 1917. The two men soon named their business the Wisconsin Farm Tractor Company. After making about 600 tractors in three horsepower sizes, production ended in 1923.

The Wisconsin tractors were rated at 16/32, 20/35, and 22/40, depending on the engines supplied with the tractors.

Looking to the Future

By no means does the above listing cover the wide spectrum of tractor manufacturers active in the 1900–1960 period. It is but a brief look at some of the better-known makers of tractors that converted farming from muscle power to motor power.

Although memory of the old machines fades with time, the contributions these machines made to that revolutionary change in farm power is being preserved. The efforts of thousands of collectors who buy them as rusting hulks, tenderly and carefully restore them, and then cherish and display them lets the rest of us appreciate the contribution those old machines made to the bountiful life we all enjoy.

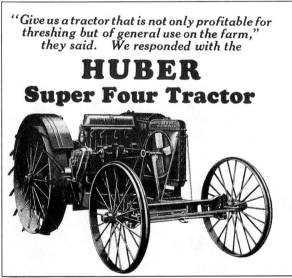

"*Give us a tractor that is not only profitable for threshing but of general use on the farm,*" *they said.   We responded with the*

HUBER
Super Four Tractor

1928 Huber 25/50

Above: *Big, surprising tractors came from Huber Manufacturing Company of Marion, Ohio. A 1929 test of the Huber 25/50 at Nebraska showed it turned out 50/60 hp, much more than expected. Rim extensions gave the 9,000-lb (4,000-kg) tractor additional flotation and grip for big drawbar pulls. This 1928 Huber 25/50 also wears a surprising color; that of World War I Olive Drab. Owner-collectors Don and Marty Huber (no relation to the original Huber) of Moline, Illinois, had the tractor repainted its original color when it was recently restored.*

Left: **1918 Huber Super Four advertisement**

The roster of orphan tractors is long, filled with makes and models well known in their time, but largely forgotten today.

The Bates Steel Mule crawler tractors were made by the Bates Machine & Tractor Company of Joliet, Illinois, and produced between 1919 and 1937.

Buffalo-Pitts Company of Buffalo, New York, did major pioneering work on threshing machines from about 1834, and produced threshers and steam and gas tractors until the early 1920s. The company's thresher design was licensed to many American makers.

Bull Tractor Company of Minneapolis was the maker of an early lightweight single-wheel-drive tractor that had a spurt of popularity between 1914 and the early 1920s.

Bullock Tractor Company of Chicago, Illinois, started in 1913, making its Creeping Grip crawler tractors from ideas and patents from the bankrupt Western Implement & Motor Company of Davenport, Iowa.

Early tractor designer Albert O. Espe of Crookston, Minnesota, made his 1907 tractor at C.O.D. Tractor Company in Crookston. Espe's designs also were used by Universal Iron Works of Stillwater, Minnesota, for its two-cylinder Universal, a machine that later became the Rumely GasPull. Espe later designed the Avery gas tractors, and was once on that firm's payroll.

Electric Wheel Company of Quincy, Illinois, a manufacturer of metal wheels, experimented with tractors beginning in 1904. In 1908, the company offered farmers a traction truck that could be converted into a farm tractor with engine mounting. By 1912, Electric Wheel sold a 15/30 Model O All-Purpose Tractor. Other models followed, and the firm continued its line of tractors until about 1930. Electric Wheel became a part of Firestone Tire & Rubber Company in 1957.

Fairbanks, Morse & Company of Chicago, Illinois, a famous maker of weighing scales, added gas engines to tractors in the late 1800s. By 1910, the firm entered the gas tractor market with machines made in Beloit, Wisconsin. The company quit making its own tractors at Beloit in 1914, but sold tractors made by other firms under its Fair-Mor name until 1918.

Gaar, Scott & Company of Richmond, Indiana, was another respected maker of steam traction engines, threshers, and sawmills. Its huge 40/70 gas tractor became the Rumely TigerPull when the M. Rumely Company bought out Gaar-Scott in 1911.

Another Indiana steam-traction engine and threshing-machine maker, Keck-Gonnerman Company of Mt. Vernon, made its first gas tractor in 1917, a two-cylinder 12/24. More standard-type models continued through the 1920s, with four-cylinder inline engine models ranging from a 18/35 up to a 30/60 "Kay Gee" Model N. Keck-Gonnerman stopped production during World War II, and did not resume manufacture after the war.

Flour City tractors came from Kinnard-Haines Company of Minneapolis beginning in 1889 and continuing until 1929 when the surviving firm, Kinnard & Sons, was bought and tractor production stopped. The Flour City machines were mostly big four-cylinder inline tractors in power sizes to 40/70.

The historic washing-machine maker, the Maytag Company of Newton, Iowa, made a farm tractor briefly in 1916. Its 12/25 tractor was produced for a short time during a period of the company's history when it offered farm implements.

A successor company to Nicolaus A. Otto, father of the four-cycle gas engine, the Otto Gas Engine Works Company made gas tractors in Philadelphia from 1896 until 1904. The company's tractors did not evolve beyond the single-cylinder stage.

John Deere grandson S. H. Velie, Jr. began the Velie Carriage Company in 1901. That Moline, Illinois, firm was followed by several Velie companies, including the Velie Motor Vehicle Company that was organized in 1908 to make autos, and the Velie Engineering Company in 1911 that specialized in trucks. The Velie firms were combined in 1916 to become Velie Motors Corporation. That company built a well-engineered tractor called the Velie Biltwell beginning in late 1916. Incorporating some of the company's automotive experience, the Biltwell had a four-cylinder inline engine of 12/24 hp. It was a standard-type tractor with automotive-type steering. Improved in 1917 with even more automotive influence, the Biltwell was discontinued in 1920 in the face of stiff competition from cheaper tractors such as the Fordson.

Yuba Ball Tread crawler tractors up to 40/70 ratings were made by the Yuba Manufacturing Company of Marysville, California, from designs originating with the Ball Tread Company of Detroit, Michigan. The Ball Tread tractor traveled on tracks running on large steel balls in a "race" under the tracks, similar in concept to a ball bearing. The design was aimed at reducing friction inherent in crawler mechanisms. The tractor used a large single wheel in front to steer the machine. The Yuba Construction Company bought the Ball Tread Company, and moved it to California in 1914. In 1918, Yuba Construction Company became Yuba Manufacturing Company. No tractors were apparently made by the firm after 1931.

Bibliography

Some of the books, periodicals, and articles used in researching this book include:

Allis-Chalmers Land Handler editors. "Partners in Productivity over 70 Years." *Allis-Chalmers Land Handler* magazine, spring 1984.

Arnold, Dave. *Vintage John Deere*. Stillwater, MN: Voyageur Press, 1995.

Broehl, Wayne G., Jr. *John Deere's Company: A History of Deere & Company and its Times*. Doubleday, 1984.

Colby, C. C. Letter dated December 2, 1946 from Colby, Equipment Sales Engineer, Oliver Industrial Division to Oliver Industrial dealers with enclosed letter to members of the American Pulpwood Assn. describing HGR-42 trials in pulpwood skidding operations.

Currie, Barton W. *The Tractor and its influence upon the agricultural implement industry*. Philadelphia: The Curtis Publishing Company, 1916.

Deere & Company. *John Deere Tractors: 1918–1994*. St. Joseph, MI: American Society of Agricultural Engineers, 1994.

Deere & Company. *The Operation, Care and Repair of Farm Machinery*. Moline, IL: John Deere, N.d.

Dingee-MacGregor. *Science of Successful Threshing*. Racine, WI: J. I. Case Threshing Machine Co., 1911.

Erb, David, and Brumbaugh, Eldon. *Full Steam Ahead: J. I. Case Tractors & Equipment 1842–1955*. St. Joseph, MI: American Society of Agricultural Engineers, 1993.

Gay, Larry. *Farm Tractors: 1975–1995*. St. Joseph, MI: American Society of Agricultural Engineers, 1995.

Gray, R. B. *The Agricultural Tractor: 1855–1950*. St. Joseph, MI: American Society of Agricultural Engineers, 1975.

Harvey, John. *Classic Tractor Collectors*. St. Joseph, MI: American Society of Agricultural Engineers, 1994.

Hoffman, Ray, and Powers, Dennis. "The 40-72 Case." *Antique Power* magazine, May-June 1995.

Johnson, Paul C. *Farm Power in the Making of America*. Wallace-Homestead, 1978.

Larsen, Lester. *Farm Tractors: 1950–1975*. St. Joseph, MI: American Society of Agricultural Engineers, 1981.

Leffingwell, Randy. *Caterpillar*. Osceola, WI: Motorbooks International, 1994.

Leffingwell, Randy. *The American Farm Tractor*. Osceola, WI: Motorbooks International, 1991.

Macmillan, Don, and Jones, Russell. *John Deere Tractors and Equipment: 1837–1959*. St. Joseph, MI: American Society of Agricultural Engineers, 1988.

Morrell, T. H. "The Development of Agricultural Equipment PTO Mechanism." St. Joseph, MI: American Society of Agricultural Engineers paper, 1980.

Prairie Farmer editors. "Farm Power From Muscle to Motor, Revolution in Rubber, Plows that Made the Prairies, The Better the Fuel . . ." *Prairie Farmer* magazine centennial issue, Jan. 11, 1941.

Strawser, Douglas. "The First Oliver Farm Tractors." *Antique Power* magazine. Nov.–Dec. 1990.

Swinford, Norm. *Allis-Chalmers Farm Equipment: 1914–1985*. St. Joseph, MI: American Society of Agricultural Engineers, 1994.

Wendel, C. H., and Morland, Andrew. *Minneapolis-Moline Tractors: 1870–1969*. Osceola, WI: Motorbooks International, 1990.

Wendel, C. H. *Encyclopedia of American Farm Tractors*. Osceola, WI: Motorbooks International, 1992.

Wendel, C. H. *International Harvester: 150 Years*. Osceola, WI: Motorbooks International, 1993.

Wik, Reynold M. *Benjamin Holt & Caterpillar: Tracks & Combines*. St. Joseph, MI: American Society of Agricultural Engineers, 1984.

Index

About the Author

Ralph W. Sanders was born and raised on a farm near Stonington, Illinois. He grew up working some of the machines tractor collectors now seek, including a Farmall F-12, Caterpillar R2, and later, a Ford-Ferguson 2N, Farmall C, and Caterpillar D2. The harvest of winter wheat in the summer and soybeans in the fall brought from the shed the 1929 Stockton, California–built Holt combine on which he and his brothers John Jr. ("Jack") and Jim took turns as "header tender." Summers also gave the Sanders boys a chance to bale hay on their grandfather Wetzel's Case wire-tie (non-automatic) pickup baler.

Rural electrification had added lights to the Old Stonington one-room country schoolhouse just before Ralph began first grade there in 1939. By the time he had completed the eighth grade, World War II was over and the Atomic Age had dawned. It was during this time that he was captivated by photography as he watched developing prints magically appear in trays spread out on the table in the darkened farmhouse's kitchen. To feed his $1.98 Kodak Baby Brownie Special camera, he stood in line for his one roll of Kodak Verichrome 127 film the day the local camera store got its monthly allotment of the precious war-rationed film.

By the time Ralph graduated from Stonington Community High School in 1951, the Korean War was underway. After studying agriculture at the University of Illinois for three years he was drafted into the U. S. Army and spent most of his two years of duty in Germany. With the help of the G.I. Bill, Ralph completed a bachelors degree in journalism at the University of Illinois, and earned his "wings"—his private pilots license.

His journalism career started with news writing and broadcasting duties at radio stations WCRA in Effingham, Illinois, and then WDZ in Decatur, Illinois. That experience led to daily newspaper reporting with the Decatur *Herald & Review,* farm reporting as Illinois field editor of *Prairie Farmer* magazine, and in 1968, more farm coverage as an associate editor at *Successful Farming* magazine in Des Moines, Iowa.

In 1974, Ralph followed his passion for photography and became a full-time freelance photographer. He then dusted off his private pilots license and, by 1978, was flying Sanders Photographics' Piper Cherokee Archer II over the eastern half of the United States on assignments for a growing number of agricultural accounts. The farm crisis of the 1980s effectively shut down "Sanders Air" and, in 1986, he sold the airplane and reluctantly joined the other "road plodders" on the highways.

Over the years, Ralph's agricultural photographic work has included assignments for *Successful Farming,* Deere & Company, Massey-Ferguson, Kinze Mfg., Vermeer Mfg., DuPont Ag, Monsanto Ag, and many others. Sanders Photographics, Inc. in Urbandale, Iowa, has grown to four employees including his wife, Joanne, and two of their sons, Scott and Richard. Ralph and Joanne have lived in West Des Moines for twenty-eight years. They have seven grown children and seven grandchildren.

Working with John Harvey, then ag division external affairs manager at DuPont, Ralph photographed the first DuPont *Classic Farm Tractors* calendar in 1990. Since then Ralph has photographed all of the *Classic Farm Tractors* calendars, covering more than one hundred tractors from all over the United States and Canada, and traveled nearly 100,000 miles in the process. Those lovingly restored tractors, originally photographed for that calendar, form the nucleus of this book. Conversations with their owners put Ralph on track to preserve some of our country's rural heritage—that of the American farm tractor.